Is Killing Peop... ....

'Great cases' are those judicial decisions around which the common law pivots. In a sequel to the instant classic *Is Eating People Wrong?*, this book presents eight new great cases from the United Kingdom, the United States and Australia. Written in a highly accessible yet rigorous style, it explores the social circumstances, institutions (lawyers, judges and courts) and ordinary people whose stories shaped the law. Across the courts' diverse and uncoordinated attempts to adapt to changing conditions and shifting demands, it shows the law as the living, breathing and down-the-street experience it really is. Including seminal cases in end of life, abortion and equal rights, this is an ideal introduction for students to legal history and jurisprudence.

Allan C. Hutchinson is a distinguished research professor at Osgoode Hall Law School, York University, and an internationally recognised legal theorist. He is the author or editor of twenty books, including *Evolution and the Common Law* (2005), *The Province of Jurisprudence Democratized* (2008) and *Is Eating People Wrong?* (2010).

Is Killing People Right?

More Great Cases That Shaped the Legal World

ALLAN C. HUTCHINSON

Osgoode Hall Law School, York University

CAMBRIDGE
UNIVERSITY PRESS

CAMBRIDGE
UNIVERSITY PRESS

32 Avenue of the Americas, New York NY 10013 2473, USA

Cambridge University Press is part of the University of Cambridge.

It furthers the University's mission by disseminating knowledge in the pursuit of education, learning, and research at the highest international levels of excellence.

www.cambridge.org
Information on this title: www.cambridge.org/9781107560888

First published 2016

Printed in the United States of America

A catalogue record for this publication is available from the British Library.

Library of Congress Cataloguing-in-Publication Data
Hutchinson, Allan C., 1951– author.
Is killing people right : more great cases that shaped the legal world /
Allan C. Hutchinson, Osgoode Hall Law School, York University.
pages cm
Includes bibliographical references and index.
ISBN 978-1-107-12386-1 (Hardback) – ISBN 978-1-107-56088-8
(Paperback)
1. Sociological jurisprudence. 2. Law–Social aspects. 3. Common law.
I. Title.
K370.H883 2016
340'.115–dc23 2015036201

ISBN 978-1-107-12386-1 Hardback
ISBN 978-1-107-56088-8 Paperback

$A2J^2$

CONTENTS

FIGURES

PREFACE

As always, I have incurred a lot of debts in writing this book. I gave lectures and seminars at a number of law schools and conferences; the feedback was most helpful and constructive. As well, I have been teaching a seminar over the past few years at Osgoode Hall, titled 'Great Cases'. I am grateful to all the students in that course for pushing me on my ideas and giving me the opportunity to refine them. Special thanks to Ian Langlois.

Most importantly, I benefitted greatly from conversations with and contributions by Adam Dodek, Trevor Farrow, Caroline Garrod, Tiffany Herbert-Ramsubick, Cynthia Hill, Jennifer Leitch, Derek Morgan, Hannah Ordman, Ronnie Tator and Emanuel Tucsa. Their critical assistance and intellectual support was invaluable. A particular thanks must go to Ian Langlois and Chris MacCormack whose industry and insight went above the call.

Finally, in researching and completing this project, I received research support from Osgoode Hall Law School.

I

INTRODUCTION

On the road (again)

That the common law is a work in progress seems beyond serious dispute. Its history is a tale of judicial innovation in the name of a better fit between law and social justice. Always travelling but never arriving, the common law is in the never-ending process of change. Any honest assessment of the common law's history, therefore, cannot fail to acknowledge that law changes over time. As such, change can be recognised as one of the few indisputable and constant facts of both life and law. As the great and Celtic Robbie Burns put it, 'Look abroad through nature's range. / Nature's mighty law is change'.

Yet, when it comes to the common law, a formidable challenge is to explain the dynamics of that change. In a world in which the common law has a relatively privileged place in channelling political power and regulating people's lives, it has to be asked and answered whether the common law is merely changing or making progress. Indeed, much of the common law's legitimacy and prestige is seen to rest upon the fact that it is not merely changing, but that it is actually improving upon itself. Once understood as a continuing work in progress, the pressing conundrum for lawyers and legal commentators becomes how to explain the tension between the need for both stability and change in the common law – what method, if any, can judges rely upon to negotiate the pushes and pulls of tradition and transformation? And to do so in a way that makes law into a better, not worse, mode of social discipline or organisation?

Despite robust disputes over the appropriate balance of these forces, there seems to exist a shared commitment to the idea that there is some elusive but enduring means or method by which to locate a workable proportion between stability and change. It is largely recognized that the past does and should matter, but there is widespread disagreement over why and how it matters – how is it possible to balance stability and continuity against flexibility and change such that it results in a state of affairs that is neither only a case of stunted development nor a case of 'anything goes'?

Eschewing any preference for revolution or stasis, most judges and jurists insist that law evolves in a measured fashion. It neither leaps forward convulsively nor stagnates idly, but advances at a slow and steady pace; it not only moves onwards, but also upwards. There is a crafty congruence posited between evolution and progress. For example, in an otherwise unexceptional judgment on personal injury damages, the future Chief Justice of Canada Beverley McLachlin gave expression to the received wisdom on how the common law evolves and progresses:

Over time, the law in any given area may change; but the process of change is a slow and incremental one based on the mechanism of extending an existing principle to new circumstances. There are sound reasons supporting this judicial reluctance to dramatically recast established rules of law. The court has before it a single case; major changes in the law should be predicated on a wider view of how the rule will operate in the broad generality of cases. Where the matter is one of a small extension of existing rules to meet the exigencies of a new case and the consequences of the change are readily assessable, judges can and should vary existing principles. But where the revision is major and its ramifications complex, the courts must proceed with great caution.

In its relatively short span, Beverly McLachlin's judgment encapsulates and highlights all the motifs of the traditional understanding of how the common law does and should work both as a general evolutionary process and as a particular resource in individual cases – incremental growth, principled extension, institutional deference, professional competence, political neutrality, cautious revision and, most importantly, progressive development. While she is attuned to the competing demands of tradition and transformation, she is convinced that some satisfactory, principled and long-term trade-off between stability and change is possible and recommended. On this view, the common law is a firmly grounded, finely balanced, ethically defensible, institutionally justified, politically legitimate and self-improving enterprise.

Yet, the occurrence of great cases and their importance in the common law process seems to defy and actually contradict this general assertion. These orienting landmarks on the common law landscape suggest that the belief in such a balancing method is more wishful thinking than anything else. The centrality of great cases to the common law strongly belies its traditional characterisation as a rational enterprise that largely has an existence of its own, is propelled forward in large part by dint of its own intellectual and moral integrity, and is always slowly fashioning itself into a better and more just body of norms. As evidenced by the importance of great cases (i.e., those cases around which legal doctrine swings and is grounded), the common law's development cannot be presented as an evolutionary stairway to juridical heaven in which the judge's role is to adopt an appropriate frame of mind, locate the first step and then confidently follow the flight secure in the expectation that it will lead somewhere good.

Instead, the common law is better understood as a rutted and rough road that has innumerable twists and turns. Crucially, it appears to have no particular final destination; any particular route taken has been chosen from among the countless and constantly proliferating possibilities for change. Efforts to provide maps or timetables for future development are unconvincing. Consequently, any comfort that traditionalists draw from the idea of evolution is cold and, therefore, misleading – there is no idea of progress that is inevitable or ingrained in the common law. Like nature, law is simply moving on largely in response to the demands and opportunities of its changing environmental situation. Neither always getting better (or worse) nor advancing in any particular direction, it is simply changing. As the science writer Carl Zimmer put it, 'evolution is change, nothing more or less'. What counts as 'progress' is as local, historical and fleeting as any other idea. Like life and law, progress itself turns out to be a work in progress.

There is little basis for lawyers' tendency to insist that the common law's evolution is weeding out the ethically bad stuff from the ethically good material. Even if they could agree on such ethical criteria, it is very hard to make a plausible case that the common law is doing this. Whether by smooth transition or jerky steps, the common law is not moving in one agreed or consistent direction. Even the most traditional commentator is prepared to concede that there are spurts and stalls in the law's development and that the supposed destination to be reached is a moving target. This is the message of great cases. Accordingly, if we are looking to locate some regimen or rule to describe and forecast the future development of the common law, then we can do no better than to subscribe to what one of Charles Darwin's colleagues termed nature's evolutionary path: 'the law of higgledy-piggledy'.

Like nature itself, the common law is a thoroughly pragmatic and piecemeal response to changing social conditions over time. It is a historical and, therefore, political endeavour in which 'anything might go'. That 'anything' rarely does 'go' is an indication not of certain natural qualities to law, but of the persistently constructed constraints of the judicial imagination that need examining for relevance and validity. Ironically (for a process that touts the virtue of constancy and predictability), it is the common law's tendency to stability rather than transformation that baffles. The fact that law changes is a given: the fact that it does so selectively and erratically is what should more engage jurists' attention and analysis.

Moreover, in the same way that a breakthrough decision or great case often occurred as a relatively revolutionary decision, so there will arise a subsequent doctrinal crisis in which what was once thought settled no longer meets contemporary demands or expectations. It is not so much that the developed doctrine will have run into internal difficulties in the sense of being found to possess latent illogicality or incoherence (although it well might). Rather, the doctrine will be seen to have outlived its substantive usefulness and be discarded for a more responsive and well-adapted set of rules and principles. It is less that the doctrine has been found to be professionally wanting from an internal standpoint and more that it has lost its political salience from an external perspective. In short, law and its particular doctrines are seen to be thoroughly political in their rise, elaboration and demise; legal tradition demands political transformation.

However, while it is reasonable to talk about progress within a particular doctrine, it seems entirely wrong-headed to do more. Talk about overall progress in the common law in the sense that a particular doctrine reaches a level of sophistication, complexity or fitness that makes it somehow perfect or even simply better for all time is silly. The history of the common law demonstrates that all such judgments about doctrinal merit and legal fairness are contingent and conditional (Chapter 6). Because law is always on the move, fixing one problem will often produce problems elsewhere, and what was once a good or adaptive solution might soon become, as the social milieu changes, a bad or maladaptive one. Whatever else it is, therefore, the common law is a work in progress that is always on the move. As such, the history of the common law is as much one of discontinuity and contingency as anything else. Like all histories, the 'progress' of the common law is best understood as a way of coping that is more or less successful in direct proportion to its capacity to achieve substantive justice in the contextual and shifting circumstances. Great cases are the best testimony to that (Chapter 4).

Legal feathers are much more ruffled by sudden switches in direction than slow accretions over time: the tortoise is the chosen symbol of the common law's development, not the hare. Yet, such a traditional 'go slowly' account of the common law (even when its injunctions are actually being heeded) has nothing to say about what is 'the best thing to do', where to go slowly or whether there are any substantive limits on change – it is all about the pace of change, not the direction of its movement. Again, the common law's progress is not channelled by law's own logic, structure or extant values. On the contrary, the common law simply works itself in line with the mediated pressures of its informing social, historical and political situation. As Brian Simpson colourfully put it, 'the point about the common law is not that everything is always in the melting pot, but that you never quite know what will go in next'. Serendipity is as much the driver of the common law as reasoned development.

As with any other human activity, it can be reported that law involves judges and lawyers making plans and acting upon them. After all, law has always been a rational activity in that people reflect upon what is best to do and how that might be achieved; it is not a game of chance or a blatant exercise of arbitrary action. But there is no 'invisible hand' that works to coordinate the scattered efforts of judicial generations. The pragmatic bent of the common law has made lawyers and judges understandably sceptical about such grand undertakings: the tentative probe is preferred to the systemic overhaul. This is largely because there is a recognition that whether a particular solution is viable or valuable will depend on the prevailing social and political milieu that is susceptible to unexpected change (Chapter 5).

Indeed, in contrast to legislation, the common law's traditional appeal is found in its relatively uncoordinated and organic character: the common law's whole is no greater than the sum of the parts, at least not on some consistent or moral basis. Over time, the quality of the common law's doctrines will occasionally move between being less and more than the sum of its parts, but it will usually be the total of its disparate parts. The common law is chaotic and coherent in relatively equal and contingently shifting measures.

Lawyers cannot claim to resolve the future of the common law as though it were only a professional or technical matter.

It involves matters of philosophy, politics, morality, economics, ideology and much more. There is a technical component, but it is more limited than lawyers would have us believe. And even technical matters are much less 'technical' than lawyers claim (Chapter 7). Working within the common law tradition is invariably a political undertaking in the sense that value choices must be made, and controversial ones at that (Chapter 2). No matter how strenuously lawyers strive to finesse these challenges, they underlie and energize all the technical work that they do. There are no easy or final answers to be discovered. More significantly, there is no method or evaluative standard that will rescue judges and lawyers from these heavy responsibilities of choice and commitment.

By understanding the common law as an organic process as much as a collection of fixed rules, it becomes possible to appreciate that good judging is about practical usefulness as much as systematic tidiness. Being a work in progress, the judicial job is never done and must console itself by accepting that this is for the best, not the worst. Nevertheless, as a work in progress, the common law dares its judicial participants to run that risk. After all, as both the best of life and law have shown, progress is what people make it. And, when it comes to the common law, what lawyers make it will be both their responsibility and their legacy. Great cases are the best testimony to that.

Because contingency is the order of the day, it has to be grasped that the quirky as much as the quotidian is the measure of development and change; yesterday's peculiar is today's prosaic and tomorrow's passé. In such a world, the common law's fabled injunction of *stare decisis et non quieta movere* (i.e., let the decision stand and do not disturb things that have been settled) seems to be an entirely misplaced and unwarranted guideline for lawyers. By relying too heavily on the past to resolve present disputes, common lawyers are likely destined to get the future wrong.

Treating the common law as a work in progress leads to the appreciation that adjudication is a subtle combination of freedom (i.e., judges can cobble together the broad range of available doctrinal materials into the artefacts of their choosing) and constraint (i.e., judges are historical creatures whose imagination and craft are bounded by their communal affiliations and personal abilities). In this way, 'anything might go'. John Donne's celebration of change as 'the nursery of music, joy, life and Eternity' better captures the kind of attitude that common lawyers should take (and the very best among them have) to their judicial duties.

Rather than resist or resent change, lawyers (and interested observers) should recognize that the strength of the common law is to be found in its invigorating willingness to keep itself open to change and to adapt as and when the circumstances require. Of course, when it is best to change and in what direction change should occur will be an inevitable matter of normative judgment: there is no manual or guidebook to follow in determining when to change or whether such change will be progressive. However, contrary to the reservations of many judges and jurists, the common law has shown that its capacity to adapt to changing circumstances is a vital feature of its historical struggle for both survival and success. Indeed, the common law seems to have been energized by recognizing the force of the old adage that 'when you are finished changing, you are finished'.

Whether particular innovations work over time will be as much a matter of serendipitous accident as deliberate design. Because the environment *will* change (and the only question is how it will change), law will also have to change in order to adapt to those changes. The search for fixed foundations or constant equations to guarantee the common law's progress is as mistaken as it is unrealisable. The best that can be hoped for is that the common law remains supple, experimental and pragmatic. Of course, in being alive to the possibilities of change, it is important for lawyers to resist the temptation to essentialise or deify change. There is no lasting or greater normative appeal to perpetual change than to perennial iner-tia: the balance between the two will be local, variable and tentative. As the history of the common law and great cases amply demonstrates, it is often possible for there to be change without improvement, but it is rarely possible for there to be improvement without change – change might be constant, but progress is contingent.

It is a compliment to the political wit and institutional savvy of common law judges that, whatever they or their apologists might say, they have largely taken a pragmatic approach to their adjudicative responsibilities; they tend not to let abstract considerations get in the way of practical solutions. This is not to suggest that the solutions they choose or the changes they make are always the best or even the better ones; this is a matter for social evaluation and political contestation. While they might mouth certain traditional platitudes about the need for predictability and stability in the common law, the judges tend to act on a quite different basis. As the iconoclastic American politician and Supreme Court justice William Douglas put it, 'the search for static security, in the law and elsewhere, is misguided ... [because] the fact is security can only be achieved through constant change, through the wise discarding of old ideas that have outlived their usefulness, and through the adapting of others to current facts'.

2

IS KILLING PEOPLE RIGHT?

Law and the end of life

The American politician Benjamin Franklin struck a truthful and lasting chord with his declaration that 'the only certain things in life are death and taxes'. While death is inevitable, its circumstances, timing and details are far from certain or predictable. It can occur at any time and almost by any means. As we manage to live longer and more securely, we have begun to demand greater control over the terms and conditions of our own death and dying; we want to avoid some of the humiliation and pain of a long and debilitating death.

Although it is no longer a criminal offence to commit suicide (even if some do consider it a sin or immoral act), many insist that they should be able to enlist the support of others to bring their life to a dignified and planned close. This, of course, has led to a whole series of moral and legal dilemmas. There is almost no approach or stance that does not receive some substantial support. For every advocate of a liberal policy on physician-assisted euthanasia there is another who condemns such possibilities as demeaning and dehumanising. It is an ethical battlefield of weighty principle and enormous implications that not only matches ethical humanists against religious devotees but also pits those in each camp against each other.

As will come with little surprise to many legal observers and social historians, the courts have been placed front and centre in this social altercation. Judges have been asked to play the role of latter-day Jobs. While the matter had bubbled under the surface for many decades, it is only in recent decades that the issue of whether and, if so, how doctors might be entitled or obliged to end a person's life has forced its way on to the front burner. The right-to-die cases are only one small corner of the wider debate on euthanasia. In the common law, the English courts were confronted by a harrowing set of circumstances in which it had to be decided if the doctors of a young and comatose victim of a monumental sporting disaster could, with his family's agreement, take him off life-support. It was a wrenching decision that placed courts squarely in the public and ethical spotlight.

AN UNSPORTING DISASTER

Tony Bland was soccer-mad. Following after his father, a warehouse worker, he was a diehard Liverpool F.C. fan. When

FIGURE 2.1. Tony Bland. Courtesy of *Liverpool Echo*

he had the chance to go to the FA Cup semi-final between Liverpool and Nottingham Forest on 15 April 1989, the 18-year-old was thrilled. Living in Keighley (which he had tattooed on one arm and 'Liverpool' on the other), it was convenient for him to make the short trip to Hillsborough Stadium in nearby Sheffield in Yorkshire, a traditional neutral venue for that semi-final game. Like a few other fans who had made the two-hour trip from Liverpool, Tony got there early on a bright spring day and lined up to get into the Lepping Lane End, which had been set aside for the Liverpool fans. Tony was in the first batch of fans to be admitted early through the turnstiles, and he made his way to the front of the terraces; it was a standing area fenced off from the pitch by an 8-foot-high steel fence that was intended to prevent pitch invasions. His particular pen had a safe capacity of around 1,600, but that day it was destined to accommodate more than 3,000.

First opened in 1899, Hillsborough had a capacity of more than 50,000. It had an unfortunate history of several crushes and collapses that resulted in injuries, but no deaths; its safety certificate had not been renewed since 1979. Expecting trouble, the local police were on high alert with such a big crowd anticipated. Indeed, as matters transpired, the police were whipped into a war mentality by Chief Superintendent David Duckenfield. He cast the Liverpool fans as a marauding army of touring drunks. A year earlier, Liverpool fans had been involved in a tragic riot at the European Cup Final when they breached a fence that separated them from Juventus fans at the Heysel Stadium in Brussels, Belgium. Thirty-nine fans, mostly supporting Juventus, were killed and 600 injured when a wall collapsed. Fourteen Liverpool fans were convicted for involuntary manslaughter, and the club was banned from European competition for ten years, later reduced to six years. Later, official inquiries ultimately exonerated Liverpool fans from all blame for the ensuing disaster and laid the responsibility squarely at the feet of the overzealous and officious police forces.

Because there were insufficient turnstiles at Hillsborough and the police were searching everyone, a backlog of fans began to develop. Fans became agitated as the 3 PM kick-off loomed. In a fateful move, the police opened a large gate ten minutes before kick-off; this gate was only intended to be opened after games to facilitate quick exits by the mass fans. Superintendent Dukenfield later told the egregious lie that the Liverpool fans had actually forced open the gate themselves. The opening of the gate allowed more fans into the already overcrowded set of terraces at the Lepping Lane End in which an unsuspecting Tony Bland was becoming increasingly sandwiched.

Six minutes after kick-off, pandemonium occurred. As fans poured in at the back of the terraces, a crash barrier collapsed near the front where Tony was standing. People began to fall on top of each other; others were squashed against the perimeter fencing. As one survivor experienced it, 'I suddenly realized that the guy next to me was dead, his eyes were bulging and his tongue [was] out. It was sheer horror. People had lost control of their bodies and the smell was horrible'. As people began to break down the fencing, the game was suspended and bodies brought out on to the field. Police and ambulance services were slow to grasp the gravity of the

FIGURE 2.2. Lepping Lane End at Hillsborough Stadium during the disaster. Courtesy of *Liverpool Echo*

situation; they maintained that this was simply more 'crowd trouble'. Bodies, dead and alive, began to accumulate on the pitch, and the full extent of the disaster was being realised. In the final accounting, there were 95 dead and more than 750 injured. All of this was caught live on national television.

Exactly what happened to Tony Bland is unclear, but he was to become the disaster's ninety-sixth and final victim. His parents, Allan and Barbara, had seen the events on TV. Not having heard from Tony by 6 PM, they made their way to Hillsborough in an agitated state. The bodies had been moved to Hillsborough's gym that was set up as an ad hoc mortuary; the bodies were photographed for identification purposes around 9 PM that evening. In the first of several controversial and crass moves, the local coroner, Stefan Popper, had the blood alcohol content of all of the bodies tested; this was orchestrated by Dukenfield and the police in efforts to shift the blame to the victims. As family members arrived, they had to identify the deceased by photograph and then, once in the gymnasium, were given only brief access to the body. As well as being questioned about their dead relatives' use of alcohol, they were also told that the bodies of the deceased were 'the property of the coroner'.

Tony Bland was simply classified as 'a missing person'. The Blands were unable to identify their son until 3 AM the next morning. By this time, he had been transferred to the Sheffield City Hospital and was in a coma. Apparently, he had been put in an ambulance on the pitch and efforts at resuscitation were made. It later transpired that, in the turmoil, Tony's ribs had been crushed and both lungs were punctured. Without oxygen, his brain suffered catastrophic and irreversible damage. He was diagnosed as being in a 'persistent vegetative state' (PVS); this meant that although his eyes were open, he had no awareness at all and had to be fed through a tube. In May, he was transferred to Airedale General in Keighley, his hometown, and put under the care of Dr Jim Howe, the head of the hospital's rehabilitation services. He was supportive of the family, but stated that 'it did not look hopeful, but we would do our best'. Every effort was made to revive him – physiotherapy, music, constant personal interaction, television and the like were tried. But it was all to little avail as a CT scan revealed cortical atrophy; he was in decline and entirely dependent on drugs and surgical intervention to remain alive.

With no change in Tony's condition by August, the family and Dr Howe began to make plans to withdraw life-supporting treatment. However, they were advised by the coroner, the same Stefan Popper, and the police that there were likely serious and potentially adverse legal consequences to such a course of action. The law was far from clear, but Dr Howe was told that such deliberate action would be tantamount to murder. While the family was undeterred in its opinion that the withdrawal of treatment was the proper and best course for their son, they refused to allow the Airedale National Health Service Trust to make an application to withdraw life-support. Still angry at the official handling of the whole Hillsborough disaster, they wanted no further involvement with the authorities or an intrusive media; they viewed Tony's fate as a personal and private matter.

The Blands continued to take care of Tony for the next three years. They were by his side every day and tried to make him as comfortable as possible. As his father said, 'Me and Barbara became institutionalized'. But, never seeing any flicker of a positive response from him, they realised that his days were numbered. In the summer of 1992, after Tony had experienced another severe infection, the family relented and agreed to let the Airedale Trust seek a declaration from the courts that would allow the withdrawal of treatment. As always, their primary goal was to relieve their son's suffering and to give him a dignified ending.

The media and public storm around the pending case was intense and emotional. The Blands and Dr Howe came under enormous pressure. Although much of the commentary was supportive, it was outweighed by the vehemence of the right-eous opposition: 'nothing and nobody on earth will be able to save you . . . from the harshest prison terms imaginable for practicing concentration camp medicine'. Indeed, one pro-life zealot, Father James Morrow, swore that he would get an arrest warrant for murder against Howe if Bland died. This all added to the pain of the Blands as they struggled to come to terms with the personal tragedy that had befallen them amidst the larger public disaster.

After a relatively quick hearing, on 19 November 1992, the President of the Family Division of the High Court, Sir Stephen Brown, found in favour of the Airedale Trust and allowed the withdrawal of life support. At the heart of the application was whether or not the artificial feeding and hydration constituted 'treatment'. If so, Dr Howe might be considered to be more starving his patient to death rather than allowing him to die: this drew upon the important but murky distinction between euthanasia and treatment withdrawal. The court's declaration stated that:

Despite the inability of the defendant to consent thereto, the plaintiff and the responsible attending physicians:

1. may lawfully discontinue all life-sustaining treatment and medical supportive measures designed to keep the defendant alive in his existing persistent vegetative state including the termination of ventilation nutrition and hydration by artificial means; and

2. may lawfully discontinue and thereafter need not furnish medical treatment to the defendant except for the sole purpose of enabling him to end his life and die peacefully with the greatest dignity and the least of pain suffering and distress;

The stage was set for the appellate courts to enter the action and make a definitive ruling on the right to withdraw life-support treatment from a comatose patient. In short order, the Court of Appeal, consisting of Sir Thomas Bingham M. R., Lady Elizabeth Butler-Sloss (the first woman ever appointed to the Court of Appeal) and Leonard Hoffman L. J., upheld the decision on 9 December 1992. However, it was left to the Judicial Committee of the House of Lords, the United Kingdom's highest court, to put their formal seal of approval on the decision and to offer an extensive and authoritative rationale. It was to prove an occasion of both considerable promise and sizeable disappointment.

A LORDLY INTERVENTION

The traditional common-law stance had been that doctors are prohibited from administering any treatment to a patient without their consent. To do otherwise would be a form of assault. This prohibition includes life-saving treatments; treating or continuing to treat a comatose or PVS patient who cannot communicate is treating a patient without consent. This situation can only be circumvented by the existence of documented orders from such a patient. In those cases where a comatose patient has explicitly left written instructions that refuse treatment, treatment cannot be administered. In cases where no instructions have been left, there is an exception where it is 'in the best interests of the patient'. Accordingly, in common-law thinking, it is not so much whether doctors withdraw the treatment of a comatose patient, but whether they may treat such patients. In *Bland*, therefore, the central issue was under what circumstances was it in a comatose patient's best interests to be treated. Earlier case law had been restricted to newborns and was indecisive.

On 4 February 1993, the House of Lords handed down its decision and upheld the Court of Appeal's decision – the withdrawal of treatment was deemed lawful and acceptable. The five law lords – Lord Keith of Kinkel, Lord Goff of Chievely, Lord Lowry of Crossgar, Lord Browne-Wilkinson of Camden and Lord Mustill of Pateley Bridge – all agreed on the outcome, but each offered a slightly different defence of why such a decision was justified as a matter of law. While the court acknowledged the primacy of the 'sanctity of life' principle, it rejected the notion that life must be preserved at all costs: life must only be preserved when such preservation is in the best interests of the patient. A PVS patient, like Tony Bland, with no hope of recovery derives no benefit as such from being kept alive; he is necessarily indifferent to matters of his own well-being. As Lord Mustill put it, 'the distressing truth which must not be shirked is that . . . the proposed conduct is not in the best interests of Anthony Bland, for he has no best interests of any kind'. Consequently, the House of

Lords held that it was not in the best interests of a conclusively diagnosed PVS patient to be artificially fed and hydrated. The best course to follow was to discontinue treatment.

Among the five judgments, Lord Goff's has come to be regarded as the leading judgment. Acknowledging that 'the sanctity of life' principle was fundamental, but not absolute, he noted that people must be allowed to determine their own fate, even if their actions appear unreasonable to others. Moreover, he drew the important distinction between withholding treatment (an omission) and administering 'a drug to his patient to bring about his death, even though that course is prompted by a humanitarian desire to end his suffering' (an act). From there, he moved to the decisive rule that the 'best interests of the patient' are primary and that it is pivotal to determine whether it is in the patient's best interests to receive continued treatment.

In Tony Bland's case, Lord Goff reached the conclusion that it was unnecessary to weigh all the relevant considerations because it cannot be in the best interests to receive medical 'treatment [that] is properly regarded as being, in medical terms, useless . . . it is the futility of the treatment which justifies its termination'. In making this extremely difficult decision about a PVS patient's best interests, Lord Goff insisted that doctors must act in accordance with 'a responsible and competent body of relevant professional opinion'. In an important qualification, he rejected the incipient American 'substituted judgment' approach of trying to ascertain what decision the patient would have made if he or she had been able to do so. For him (and his colleagues), this was too contrived and speculative.

Nevertheless, although allowing the withdrawal of treatment for Tony, the judges all agonised over the moral dilemmas and unresolved conundrums that accompanied their decision. They made a concerted pitch for legislative intervention. For instance, Lord Lowry was alert to the observation that there is 'a possible gap . . . between old law and new medicine and perhaps also, I might add, new ethics'. Again, Lord Mustill captures the discomfort of his colleagues in reaching a conclusion that puts a doctor with a PVS patient who is unable to consent in a better position than one who ends the life of a consenting patient. Whereas the latter commits murder, the former is absolved from full responsibility for her action. Indeed, Lord Mustill seems to speak for most lawyers and judges when he notes that:

> The acute unease which I feel about adopting this way through the legal and ethical maze is I believe due in an important part to the sensation that, however much the terminologies may differ, the ethical status of the two courses of action is for all relevant purposes indistinguishable. By dismissing this appeal, I fear that your Lordships' House may only emphasise the distortions of a legal structure that is already both morally and intellectually misshapen. Still, the law is there and we must take it as it stands.

A HEATED REACTION

Of course, although the House of Lord's decision brought clarity to Tony Bland's situation, it simply ended one controversy by opening a whole new set of conversations about other related matters and contexts. But this is the way of the common law; the law develops by leaps and sometimes bounds out of one quandary and into another. The ruling was met by a predictable barrage both inside and outside the legal community as well as across the common law world. Such is the pertinence and persistence of the underlying normative debate on the right-to-die that it is unrealistic to imagine that any legal decision can bring it to a satisfactory or ultimate conclusion. However, the decision received more compliments than condemnations.

Representative of the positive response was the reflections of Peter Singer, a celebrated Australian ethical philosopher with a reputation for uncompromising views. He made much of the fact that *Bland* had broken new ground by establishing in law the important idea that 'quality of life' was a decisive factor in deciding whether a life should be continued: the worth of a person's life must be weighed against its mere biological existence. However, he was sceptical about the pivotal distinction between acts (i.e., killing) and omissions (i.e., letting die). Even if it was conceptually defensible, he challenged its moral relevance. He concluded by noting that, while the law lords did the best they could in the circumstances, their decision was 'morally incoherent' and cried out for 'a new approach to life-and-death decisions' to be taken by elected politicians.

Richard Huxtable, a clinical ethicist, was less charitable. Although he did not condemn the actual outcome, he was more troubled by the judgments' confused and confusing arguments. Emphasising the general intellectual inconsistency of the law resulting from *Bland*, he took the law lords to task for being unclear about why it ever should be lawful to end life intentionally. Huxtable agreed with the conclusion of Roger Magnusson, a Sydney lawyer:

> In their eagerness to distinguish euthanasia, the Law Lords camouflaged the central issue: whether withdrawing life-support and so ending a patient's life was justified in the circumstances. It is better to see the withdrawal of life-preserving treatment for what it is: *a form of non-voluntary euthanasia*, and to justify it on ethical or policy grounds, than to pretend that doctors are not, by withdrawing life-support from an incompetent patient dependent on it, engaged in the killing business.

In 1999, the British Medical Association published its own guidelines; these glossed the *Bland* position. They permitted the withdrawal of tube feeding from certain non-PVS patients on the basis that 'the BMA can see no reason to differentiate between decisions for patients in PVS and those for patients with other serious conditions (e.g., stroke or dementia)'. Moreover, the BMA took the bold step of advising doctors that there was no need to seek legal declarations in such instances. These guidelines were incorporated in principle, if not by wording, in the *Mental Capacity Act* of 2005. Intended to offer a comprehensive statutory regime, it followed the *Bland* lead. In the case of mentally incapacitated adults, the primary consideration was to be 'the best interests of the patient'; a patient's earlier expressed views and values should inform such an evaluation. An important innovation was to establish a Court of Protection with jurisdiction over the financial and welfare decisions of people who lacked the mental capacity to make these decisions for themselves.

In regard to *Bland*, the most important decision to be made by the new Court of Protection was in the case of *Re M.* in 2011. A middle-aged woman fell into a coma. She was not considered to be a PVS patient because she still had some minimal consciousness and self-awareness. For the Court, Justice Baker rejected the argument that withdrawal can never be in the patient's best interests. Instead, he preferred the 'balance sheet' approach in which all relevant factors (e.g., the patient's past wishes, prospects of recovery, dignity, family preferences, etc.) must be considered. On the particular facts, it was held that it was not in M.'s best interests for treatment to be withdrawn: her continuing treatment was a matter of clinical discretion, and the decision whether to withdraw treatment could be revisited if her condition changed.

Of course, other common law jurisdictions have grappled with the legal and moral dilemmas of withholding treatment from incapacitated patients. In the United States, for instance, the courts have held that in dealing with PVS patients like Tony Bland, the central task is to ascertain evidence that the patient would not have wished to be kept alive. The most prominent case is *Cruzan* in 1990. Nancy Cruzan was in a car accident in 1983; her brain was deprived of oxygen for twelve to fourteen minutes. After being in a coma for three weeks, she was eventually diagnosed as being a PVS patient. Her parents sought to withdraw artificial nutrition and hydration on the basis that Nancy had earlier confided to a former housemate that she would not want to live if she were so ill or injured as to be unable to lead a life 'at least halfway normally'. Although the Missouri trial court gave authorisation to do so, that decision was overturned on appeal. The case was framed at the US Supreme Court in terms of whether the relevant Missouri law, which required 'clear and convincing evidence' of the incapacitated individual's wishes in such circumstances, contravened Nancy's liberty interest under the US Constitution's 'due process' clause.

In Chief Justice Rehnquist's majority judgment, it was accepted that there was both a common law and constitutional right to refuse treatment. However, it was held that the state had a legitimate interest in the preservation of life and that it was reasonable for the state to put higher-than-normal safeguards in place when determining what the deceased wanted or would have wanted in the event of being incapacitated. Accordingly, the Missouri law was upheld and Nancy's desire to have treatment withheld was not sufficiently demonstrated. Moreover, the wishes of the family were not considered to be conclusive in themselves because they could not always be trusted to act in the best interests of the incompetent patient. This represents a very different approach to the English courts' balance-sheet analysis.

The Supreme Court of Canada has hinted at how it might proceed in such matters in its recent decision in *Rasouli*. An attending physician sought to remove life support and provide palliative care to an unconscious patient because all appropriate treatments had been exhausted and the continuation of life support offered no medical benefit. This approach was resisted by the patient's wife. Under prevailing legislation, the Court decided that the withdrawal of life support amounted to treatment under the Act and therefore required consent. However, it was appropriate for the legislatively created administrative board to decide if the patent's wife was acting in the patient's interest in refusing her consent. Although by no means conclusive in its decision, the court showed a definite preference for the English approach and for patients' best interests to be the standard, not their intuited intentions.

Therefore, common law courts have struggled with right-to-die cases. Whether adopting a 'best interests' or 'expressed intentions' stance, judges are placed in an invidious position. However, the difficulties of the American approach are made manifest by the *Schiavo* case. A PVS patient's family disagreed about whether she had expressed a clear desire to have treatment withheld if she fell into a coma. During tortuous efforts to determine her wishes – fourteen appeals and numerous hearings in the Florida courts, five suits in federal district court, Florida legislation struck down, federal legislation (the Palm Sunday Compromise) and four denials of *certiorari* (leave to appeal) from the US Supreme Court – she was kept alive for over fourteen years before her feeding tube was finally removed. This hardly seems the most sensible, let alone humane, way to ensure a dignified life or death.

A TRAGEDY REVISITED

The personal tragedy of the Bland family finally came to an end almost four years after the horrendous events at Hillsborough. A couple of weeks after the House of Lords made its decision, Tony's life-support measures were stopped and he died a miserable eight days later of bronchopneumonia on 3 March 1993. He had been visited by members of the Liverpool team; this was the only time that he 'met' his heroes. His parents, Allan and Barbara, maintained that Tony had died at Hillsborough and that what had followed was all unnecessary and, as Dr Howe said, was 'an affront to his dignity'. His

FIGURE 2.3. Banner at Liverpool F.C. match, in remembrance of Tony Bland and the other victims. Courtesy of *Liverpool Echo*

father has always insisted that, faced with similar circumstances, 'I'd do exactly the same again'. Along with their daughter, Angela, the Blands remain involved in the right-to-die movement.

The larger consequences of the Hillsborough disaster still drag on almost twenty-five years later. Not only does it remain a heart-rending chapter in football's colourful history but it also became a social and political issue of lasting significance. Immediately after the disaster, a public inquiry was launched under the leadership of Lord Chief Justice Peter Taylor. In its final report, it was concluded that the main cause of the dreadful mayhem was 'a failure of police crowd control': the police were inadequately briefed, took an adversarial stance against Liverpool supporters and engaged in a deplorable cover-up after the event. Henceforth, all standing terraces were removed from major football stadiums in the United Kingdom and live TV coverage of such tragedies was suitably modified. Also, private prosecutions for manslaughter were brought against Chief Superintendent David Duckenfield and his deputy, Superintendent Bernard Murray. They went on trial in 2000. While Murray was acquitted, the jury could not reach a verdict on Duckenfield. However, much to many people's anger, a retrial was not pursued on the basis that 'Mr. Duckenfield had faced public humiliation and a fair trial would be impossible'.

But the public outcry about the disaster did not abate. In 2009, a parent of a Hillsborough victim, Anne Williams, lost a case at the European Court of Human Rights; she sought to get documents released and the inquest reopened. However, it did manage to reignite the still smouldering demands for a full and new inquiry to establish if there had been a deliberate official cover-up. After the twentieth anniversary of the disaster in April 2009, the Labour Government announced the creation of the Hillsborough Independent Panel, chaired by the Bishop of Liverpool, James Jones. The panel was tasked with 'full public disclosure of all relevant information' and adequate consultation with the Hillsborough families who had been effectively frozen out of earlier inquiries. In September 2012, the Panel concluded that 41 of the 96 deaths might have been averted, that 164 witness statements had been altered, that 116 statements unfavourable to the police had gone missing, and that the original inquest verdicts of 'accidental death' be reopened. The sad saga continues.

The great and late Liverpool manager, Bill Shankly, had once uttered his famous response to a reporter's question about whether or not football was a matter of life and death, saying 'it's much more important than that'. He may well have revised his view if he had witnessed the Hillsborough disaster.

Flames were added to the Liverpool F.C. crest in memory of those who died at Hillsborough. Nevertheless, the football season continued and Liverpool suffered the usual triumphs and agonies. After beating Nottingham Forest in the rearranged semi-final, it won the final 3–2 after extra time in a fitting close encounter with its local neighbours, Everton. However, it lost the league title to Arsenal in the final minute of the final game of the 1988–89 season. Tony Bland would have relished being at both events. He would have cheered and cried along with the thousands of others. The emotional anthem, 'You'll Never Walk Alone', resonates as a moving weekly ritual sung by Liverpool fans on behalf of Tony Bland and their lost colleagues.

CONCLUSION

There are no easy or uncontroversial answers to the right-to-die cases. Indeed, the storm in this area of the law does not augur well for the wider debate on euthanasia that is brewing. For instance, another Hillsborough victim, Andrew Devine, was diagnosed as being a PVS patient. His parents did not want him to be taken off life support, and as of this writing he remains alive in a minimally conscious state. The fates of both Tony Bland and Andrew Devine testify to the wrenching dilemmas of the right-to-die issue. Perhaps the crafted words of Oscar Wilde's *The Ballad of Reading Gaol* offer a fitting, if controversial, challenge to those who ponder the life-and-death debate and have to act on behalf of their loved ones:

> Yet each man kills the thing he loves,
> By each let this be heard,
> Some do it with a bitter look,
> Some with a flattering word,
> The coward does it with a kiss,
> The brave man with sword.

3

OIL ON TROUBLED WATERS

The consequences of civil liability

Everyone makes mistakes or acts carelessly. Most of the time, the error is harmless and life goes on much as normal. But, at other times, a small slip can result in large and harmful consequences; injuries can be widespread and damage can be catastrophic. While the common law has long had a set of rules that holds careless individuals responsible for their negligent acts, it continues to wrestle with the thorny question of whether they should be liable for all or only some of the damage that they cause. For example, someone might inadvertently drop a still-lit cigarette stub in a waste bin that results in a fire that burns down a whole district and kills many people. In legal doctrine, this is known as 'the remoteness of damage' problem.

For many, this distinction between the nature of the act done and the extent of damage caused by it may appear contrived and almost beside the point. It might be claimed that people should have a moral obligation to assume the full costs and consequences of their blameworthy actions, even if the extent of damage was unexpected; the law should effect and mirror such a stance. However, for the last fifty years or so, the common law has taken seriously the argument that there should be some proportionality between the nature of the careless act and the extent of liability for its consequences; small acts of negligence should give rise to smaller liability than larger ones. As with much else, 'reasonableness' is the watchword of the common law of tort.

The leading cases on remoteness of damage, each flowing from the same shipping incident in Sydney Harbour, occurred in the mid-twentieth century. Like so many of the common law's great cases, the surrounding circumstances and characters involved as well as the social attitudes displayed were very much in line with the times. However, since then, values and sensitivities have changed. Even though the guiding principles of law remain the same today, it is not too difficult to appreciate that a similar set of facts might well produce a different outcome today. And perhaps that is as it should be – the common law shifts and switches with the prevailing social milieu; it moves, not in lock step, but along much the same path, often lagging behind, but occasionally pulling ahead. Moreover, the leading cases played out in a way that will have some onlookers marvelling at the convoluted and almost downright ridiculousness of certain legal doctrines.

SPARKS AND SPILLS

If Australia is considered to be God's Own Country by its locals, then Sydney Harbour is its centrepiece. An imposing and physically striking area, it is an inlet of the southern Pacific Ocean. Originally a drowned river valley, it stretches almost 19 kilometres inland and has a coastline of over 315 kilometres. Yet for all its natural beauty and built attractions (e.g., the Harbour Bridge and Opera House) it was also the hub of Australia's vital and wealth-generating fledging industries; heavy engineering, oil refining and general maritime facilities grew up around the inner harbour. At its heart was the waterside western suburb of Balmain. Home to Australia's first union movement and the political Labour Party in the late nineteenth century, it has been justly celebrated as 'the birthplace of modern industry in Australia'.

The first steam ships began to appear in Sydney Harbour in 1853. It was clear that it would not be long before docking and general repair facilities were needed. Thomas Sutcliffe

Mort was a man who always had an eye for the entrepreneurial chance and saw great opportunity in the opening up of the new southern continent. He had arrived in Sydney around 1830. Born in 1816 and raised modestly around Manchester, England, he was a man of vigour and innovation. His lasting claim to fame was his contribution to improving the refrigeration of meat. However, he diversified his interests and managed to build a considerable personal fortune. While he lived a relatively extravagant life, he remained popular by his willingness to share some of his wealth with the local community. He opened up his Darling Point mansion and gardens to the public and offered shares in his companies to their employees. Thomas Mort was a go-getter.

Along with J. S. Mitchell and Captain Thomas Rountree, Mort invested in the first dry dock in Australia, let alone Sydney, in 1855. It was located on the former Strathean Estate on Waterview Bay in Balmain. But, by the mid-1860s, docking was no longer so profitable due to stiff competition from other neighbouring docks; a large part of the dock became leased for cargo storage and engineering works. To take advantage of this, Mort developed a marine and general engineering business. As well as manufacturing and repairing ships, the business also assembled imported locomotives and made water pipes. In 1872, *Mort's Dock & Engineering Company* was formed; Mort left the day-to-day management of the company to James Franki who remained in charge for an astonishing fifty years until his retirement in 1922. The company became the largest private firm in the new colony of New South Wales and its second largest employer. On Mort's death in 1878, the Mayor of Balmain, James McDonald, and the local council renamed the bay 'Mort's Bay' in honour of its local industrial hero.

In the ensuing years, the fortunes of Mort's Dock & Engineering Company ebbed and flowed. It was busy and profitable during the Second World War when it won several military contracts and built multipurpose vessels for the Australian Navy. However, after the War, the company fell on harder times; shipbuilding declined generally and many

FIGURE 3.1. Mort's Dock, 1941. Australian War Memorial,
www.awm.gov.au/collection/009316/.

competitors moved to cheaper premises on the western shores
of Sydney Harbour. By 1951, the dock was used to maintain
and repair smaller ships. It was also known as Sheerlegs
Wharf, and it was situated across from a growing set of docks
for unloading oil.

Overseas Tankship Limited was a UK-based tanker company. It had been formed in 1950 by Caltex and was jointly
owned by Texaco and Chevron, two large American corporations. It had about thirty tankers in its fleet; most were Second
World War, American-designed and-built T2 tankers. One of
its vessels was the *S.S. Wagon Mound*; this was a 10,172-tonne
oil-burning vessel that was built in 1945. It spent most of its
time carrying crude oil between oil fields in the Middle East
and Australia where it was refined for commercial use. In late
October 1951, it berthed at the Caltex Wharf on Ballast Point
(now a recreational park); it was about 600 feet across from
Sheerlegs Wharf in the adjoining Mort Bay. She was only there
for a little over twenty-four hours, but in that time not only
managed to spill a considerable quantity of oil but also gave
rise to a lawsuit that would reshape the common law.

Early in the morning of 29 October, the *Wagon Mound* docked at the Caltex Jetty in Mort's Bay. It was there to discharge its cargo of petrol to be refined by Caltex and to take on bunkering or furnace oil. During this procedure, a significant amount of bunkering oil was allowed to overflow in the harbour; this was caused by the undisputed negligence of the *Wagon Mound*'s crew. By the next morning, the oil had spread across the harbour in the direction of Mort Dock's Sheerlegs Wharf: it was concentrated in thick slicks around the Wharf. No effort was made by the *Wagon Mound* or Caltex to clean up the spill. Less than twenty-six hours after its arrival, the *Wagon Mound* set sail and left Sydney Harbour at 11:00 a.m. on 30 October. It was then that trouble and further damage began to occur.

When workers arrived at Mort's Dock on the morning of 30 October, they were prepared to continue working on the refit of two ships owned by the Miller Steamship Company – the *S.S. Corrimal* and *S.S. Audrey D.* As the day's work was to involve oxyacetylene welding (which could generate temperatures as high as 3,000°C), the wharf manager, Mr Parkin, decided that there should be no further activity until the precise fire risk of the congealed oil was clarified. To this end, he contacted a Mr Durack at Caltex where the Wagon mound

FIGURE 3.2. The *S.S. Wagon Mound.* www.aukevisser.nl/ t2tanker/id228.htm

had discharged its cargo. Mr Durack came over to the Sheerlegs Wharf and assured Mr Parkin that the oil was not a fire hazard because its presumed flash point of 170°F made ignition on water 'close to impossible'. The Mort Dock's workers restarted their welding by mid-morning. Out of an abundance of caution, the welders were given strict instructions that all safety precautions should be taken so as to prevent inflammable material falling off the wharf onto the oil.

Welding continued for the rest of the day without incident. However, the next day, signs that all was not well were glimpsed. Around 2:00 p.m. on Thursday, 1 November, two boilermakers, a Mr McGiffen and a Mr Godfrey, were working on the *Corrimal* and saw a small flame beginning to burn and grow in size on a piece of bark that was floating on top of the oil. It was later established that this had acted as a 'wick'. In short order, the flame set fire to a pile of debris. This, in turn, ignited the oil and a substantial conflagration followed. The wharf was burned down and the *Corrimal*, a 230-foot steamship, was severely damaged; all workers were able to escape with very few injuries. The fire could be seen all across the harbour. Mr Durack telephoned Mr Parkin and exclaimed, 'Good Lord, your place has gone up in flames.' The damage was considered to be around $100,000 in total.

It was soon clear that there would be no easy or quick resolution of the matter. Mort's Dock insisted that the owners of the *Wagon Mound* had not only been careless in allowing the initial oil spill, but also that they had been negligent in failing to clean up after themselves and in failing to warn Mort's Dock of the dangers associated with the build-up of bunkering oil around the wharf. In response, the *Wagon Mound* denied each and every allegation in the plaintiff's statement of claim. They contended that 'furnace oil floating on water is not highly or easily inflammable and can be ignited only by some burning substance coming in contact therewith capable of acting as a wick' and, as a result, the fire and resulting damage was unforeseeable. Moreover, they argued, in the alternative (as it is possible to do so, even if one line of argument contradicts the other), that the primary cause of the fire was Mort Dock's own negligence in continuing to weld while being aware that oil was underneath the wharf. So organized in opposition, the case was destined to become heated and contested.

A QUESTION OF REASONABLENESS

In English and Commonwealth law at the time, a negligent party was only responsible for those damages that it actually caused. While this was a fairly uncontentious issue, it was often unclear what the test for 'causation' was and whether it had been satisfied in the specific circumstances of a case. This was particularly so where there was some intervening act between one party's negligence and another's damage. Notwithstanding this, the courts also conditioned an injured party's success on whether it could be shown that the damage caused was not too remote. Again, while this condition was firmly entrenched in the law of torts, the meaning and scope of 'remoteness' was far from certain.

The trail took place in the Superior Court of New South Wales in February and March 1958. After a hearing of several days, Justice Kinsella reserved his judgment until 23 April 1958. In a wide-ranging and thorough judgment, he made several important findings of fact and law. Importantly, he relied extensively on the testimony and scientific tests of Professor Hunter, a distinguished researcher in chemical engineering at Sydney University and an internationally renowned expert on oil's inflammability. It was held that it was not foreseeable that bunkering oil would ignite in the circumstances of the case: 'the *raison d'être* of furnace oil is, of course, that it shall burn, but I find the defendant did not know and could not reasonably be expected to have known that it was capable of being set afire when spread on water'. Nevertheless, Justice Kinsella found in favour of Mort's Dock because the legal test for remoteness, as established in the 1921 English Court of Appeal decision of *Re Polemis*, was simply whether damage to Mort's Dock by the *Wagon Mound*'s negligence was directly caused: 'directness of causation is the sole criterion of recoverability'. Damages of $90,000 in total were awarded to Mort's Dock for the harm caused to its facilities and operations.

Overseas Tankship appealed on the basis that Kinsella had applied the wrong legal test – the test for remoteness was or should be the 'reasonable foreseeability' of the damage, not 'all the direct consequences' of the negligent act. In a decision by Justices Owen, Maguire and Manning, the court dismissed the appeal and upheld the judgment of Justice Kinsella. Although unpersuaded by the inherent wisdom of the 'all the direct consequences' test in *Re Polemis*, the court felt obliged to follow it as a matter of ruling precedent. In a tour de force, Justice Manning found in favour of Mort's Dock, but offered a plea for clarity from appellate courts:

to say that the problems, doubts and difficulties ... render it difficult for me to apply the decision in *Re Polemis* with any degree of confidence ... would be a grave under-statement. I can only express the hope that ... the subject will be pronounced upon by the House of Lords or the Privy Council.

As was still the practice in the late 1950s, there could be an appeal from the Australian state courts directly to the Privy Council in London. This body was essentially the same court as the Judicial Committee of the House of Lords: this vestige of colonialism was finally extinguished in the mid-1980s. In the *Wagon Mound* case, there was a bench of five senior law lords – Viscount Simonds of Sparsholt, Lord Reid of Drem, Lord Radcliffe of Werneth, Lord Tucker of Great Bookham and Lord Morris of Borth-y-Gest. As was the Privy Council's tradition, one opinion was given on 18 January 1961; it was authored by Viscount Simonds. It turned around the Australian decisions, formulated a new doctrine of remoteness and found against Mort's Dock. It was a legal ruling of staunch, if dubious and cloudy, principle. It managed to offer greater clarity in part and greater confusion in part.

Gavin Simonds was the scion of a brewing family dynasty. His father, Louis De Luze Simonds, had been living in New York, but returned to England in 1872 to take up the reins of the company and later became its Managing Director. *H & G. Simonds* had been founded in 1785 and had come to fame as purveyors to the English army and as the originators of the still going strong India Pale Ale; it became part of the Courage label in 1960 and was subsequently absorbed by the massive Newcastle and Scottish breweries. Born in Reading in November 1881, Gavin's destiny was to bring a much-needed respectability and refinement to the family. This he did with distinction. After a traditional education at Winchester and Oxford, he became a barrister in 1906 and was appointed a King's Counsel in 1924. After being made a judge in 1937, he soon made it to the House of Lords in 1944. In 1951, he was named Lord Chancellor; this made him the head of the judiciary and a member of Churchill's cabinet. Retiring in 1962, he outlived his three sons, two of whom died on active military service. Although his life peerage came to end with his death in June 1971 at the age of 89, he had come a long way from the humble roots of his beer-making ancestors.

In his opinion in the *Wagon Mound* case, Viscount Simonds provided an exhaustive survey of the case law leading up to *Re Polemis* and its later judicial treatment and scholarly reception. He came to the decisive conclusion that its precedential authority 'has been severely shaken though lip-service has from time to time been paid to it'. Moreover, he was of the strong view that the 'direct consequences' rule 'leads to a conclusion equally illogical and unjust'. Having cleared away the doctrinal hold of the 'direct consequences' test, he proceeded to offer a more compelling, substantive rationale for why the 'reasonable foreseeability' standard was more suited to the remoteness issue specifically and modern negligence liability generally.

Viscount Simonds emphasized that, since 1921 and especially after *Donoghue v. Stevenson* in 1932 (the Snail-in-the-ginger-beer case), tort law had become more fully anchored around the concept of 'reasonable foreseeability' as the standard for establishing tort liability: 'it is the foresight of the reasonable man which alone can determine responsibility'. Consequently, he insisted that it was entirely fitting that there should be an intellectual symmetry – the same standard should be employed to measure both the basis of liability for negligent acts and the extent of that liability for the act's resulting consequences:

For it does not seem consonant with current ideas of justice or morality that for an act of negligence, however slight or venial, which results in some trivial foreseeable damage the actor should be liable for all consequences however unforeseeable and however grave, so long as they can be said to be 'direct'. It is a principle of civil liability, subject only to qualifications that have no present relevance, that a man must be considered to be responsible for the probable consequences of his act. To demand more of him is too harsh a rule, to demand less is to ignore that civilised order requires the observance of a minimum standard of behaviour.

As Justice Kinsella had found as a fact that a fire resulting from the particular oil spillage from the *Wagon Mound* was not reasonably foreseeable, this meant that Mort's Dock lost their case and received no compensation for the damage caused by the fire. Although Overseas Tankship had committed a serious act of negligence in allowing oil to escape from the *Wagon Mound* (and had left the harbour without any attempt to clean up the spill), they were not liable for its harmful, but 'remote' consequences. While little mention was made of it by the Privy Council, it was not unimportant that it was the actions of Mort's Dock itself in resuming welding, albeit on supposedly reassuring professional advice from the oil company, that had been the immediate cause of the fire. The question that continues to haunt the common law is whether such a ruling and its application is, to echo Viscount Simond's words, 'consonant with current ideas of justice or morality' Because the 'current morality' of the 1950s is not the same as that of the 2010s, would the outcome be different today?

A FORESEEABLE CONSEQUENCE?

Since 1961, judges of the common law have striven to develop and elaborate upon the meaning of the reasonable foreseeability test. They have tried to develop a measure for calculating the kind of injuries and harm for which a negligent actor is responsible. This has proved to be a difficult, if not sleeveless errand. As always, the courts have made little distinction between large corporations, like Overseas Tankship, and the law's 'reasonable man'; it seems unrealistic to evaluate the liability of massive and highly profitable organizations as if they were one-man operations. Nevertheless, the law has tended to hold with the general applicability of the 'reasonable foreseeability' test but to apply it flexibly in line with changing social and political mores. Indeed, it is doubtful today if an oil-spilling ship (that upped and left without any effort to clean-up) would be treated quite so favourably as the *Wagon Mound*.

For instance, in a subsequent series of cases, it had to be decided if the long-standing rule that negligent actors take their victims as they find them remained in force – if a victim has a particular and unusual vulnerability (e.g., haemophilia), can they still recover for a high level of injury (e.g., bleeding to death) that would not be experienced by an average person? Known as the 'thin-skull' rule, the common law allowed for full recovery in such circumstances. In the 1962 case of *Smith v. Leech Brain*, Chief Justice Parker of the English Court of Appeal held that Viscount Simonds could not have intended that this rule be swept aside. Accordingly, it remained the case that all that was necessary for recovery was to show that the type of injury to the victim could be reasonably foreseen, not its extent. Also, it was later decided in 1963 in *Hughes* that, as long as the type of injury could be foreseen, it was not necessary that the precise way in which it occurred could be foreseen. In effect, the courts began to soften the harshness of a strict application of the *Wagon Mound* decision.

Another challenge for the courts was to decide what to do about so-called intervening acts; this is what the law calls the doctrine of *novus actus interveniens*. For example, if owners negligently leave their keys in their car and someone drives off with their car, would the owners be liable for any injuries to other people if their car was in an accident? Courts have gone back and forth on this matter. The general response has been to impose liability, but in increasingly restricted circumstances. The original rule, following the logic of the *Wagon Mound*, was that a negligent person was liable for any reasonably foreseeable intervening act by an unknown or unavailable third person. However, judges have cavilled at imposing too much liability in such tenuous circumstances. In recent years, the judges have resiled from the reasonably foreseeable test as 'producing some astonishing results'. Instead, they have favoured a rule that would only impose liability for intervening acts where there was 'a degree of likelihood amounting almost to inevitability'.

However, although the *Wagon Mound* brought to an end the claim of Mort's Docks, it did not end the litigation resulting from the oil spill fire. In a case that has come to be known as *Wagon Mound (No 2)*, the owners of the *Corrimal*, Miller Steamship, sued Overseas Tankship for damage to its ship resulting from the fire caused by the oil spill from the *Wagon Mound*. The outcome of that case offers telling insights not only about remoteness of damage, but several other important legal doctrines of a more procedural nature. While the law from earlier cases binds later cases (*stare decisis*), the facts found in earlier cases do not bind later cases unless the same parties are involved (*res judicata*). *Wagon Mound (No 2)* tested the limits of those two doctrines.

Although the general facts were much the same, the trial judge in *Wagon Mound (No 2)* made some small but different findings of facts that were vital; the findings of Justice Kinsella in *Wagon Mound (No 1)* were not binding, as it was Miller Steamship, not Mort's Dock, that brought the case. Most importantly, Justice Walsh determined after hearing all the evidence that 'reasonable people ... would regard furnace oil as very difficult to ignite upon water' and that the risk of fire was 'a possibility, but one which could become an actuality only in very exceptional circumstances'. When the case finally reached the Privy Council again in May 1966, almost fifteen years after the actual fire, this was enough to trigger a decision in favour of Miller Steamship.

Lord Reid (who, along with Lord Morris had sat on the earlier *Wagon Mound* decision) gave the opinion of the Privy Council. He began by emphasizing that the 'reasonable fore-seeability' test laid down in *Wagon Mound* in 1961 was not only binding as a matter of formal precedent, but also made good sense as a matter of substantive fairness. When he combined this with the slightly different factual findings of Justice Walsh (i.e., that there was a possible, if remote, risk of fire), Lord Reid and his colleagues came to the conclusion that the *Wagon Mound*'s engineers should not have neglected to make a reasonable effort at cleaning up the oil spillage to eliminate or reduce the small risk of fire:

> If a real risk is one which would occur to the mind of a reasonable man in the position of the defendant's servant and which he would not brush aside as far-fetched and if the criterion is to be what that reasonable man would have done in the circumstances, then surely he would not neglect such a risk if action to eliminate it presented no difficulty, involved no disadvantage, and required no expense.

While Miller Steamship was jubilant, Mort's Dock might be forgiven for thinking that it had got a raw deal. Indeed, the operation of the doctrines of *stare decisis* and *res judicata* in tandem might be thought to confirm Mr Bumble's assessment in Charles Dickens's *Oliver Twist* that 'the law is an ass – an idiot'. While Mort's Dock had failed to recover damages for harm to its property, the owners of the ships on which its employees had been working did recover from exactly the same negligently caused fire; this seemed to add legal insult to personal injury. However, the fact was that, while the relevant legal doctrines were not entirely 'idiotic' (at least when considered separately), Mort's Dock was no longer in business by the time the Privy Council handed down its decision in 1966.

Overseas Tankship was unaffected by the litigation and continued to operate until the 1990s. The *Wagon Mound* itself sailed the world with its lucrative cargo for the next ten years: it was finally scrapped in Kaohsiung, Taiwan, in September 1969. However, the sad fact was that the almost century-old

FIGURE 3.3. Mort Bay Park, Balmain in 2013, site of Mort's Dock.
Wikimedia Commons, https://commons.wikimedia.org/wiki/
File:1._east_balmain_park_on_mort_bay_syd_harbour.jpg.

Mort's Dock & Engineering was far from being in good financial health as the *Wagon Mound* litigation wended its long way through the courts. In the first six months of 1956, the company lost £177,644 as a result of labour troubles. It closed its operations at Sheerlegs Wharf in November 1958 and went into liquidation in 1959; it ceased trading completely in 1968. The Dock was soon demolished and converted into a container storage terminal for ships. However, in 1989, the site was transformed from a container storage terminal into a waterfront park as part of the general gentrification of the Balmain suburb. Yet, the nearby 'Dry Dock Hotel' still stands as a commemorative and old-world symbol of the area's rich history from the heyday of the shipbuilding industry in Sydney Harbour. On 17 January 2011, NSW's Planning Minister, Tony Kelly, declared Mort's Dock to be a State Heritage Site.

CONCLUSION

The courts still hold to the reasonable foreseeability test, even as they struggle to give it clear and practical effect. Very recently, there was a Canadian case that both confirmed the force of the *Wagon Mound* principle of reasonable foreseeability and its limitations. In *Mustapha*, a man saw a dead fly in a large flagon of filtered water that he had purchased. Although he did not drink any water from the bottle, he suffered a psychological breakdown as a result of the fact that he already had a very serious disposition of mental anxiety in regard to issues of dirt and cleanliness. The Supreme Court of Canada decided that there could be no recovery against the bottling company because the damage caused was too remote. As it was not foreseeable that 'a person of ordinary fortitude' would suffer any injury or harm from the incident, the thin-skull rule did not come into play; the type of harm was not reasonably foreseeable, so the unanticipated extent of the harm was not a relevant factor. Opinion remains divided about whether this outcome was either fair or followed from the *Wagon Mound* principle.

Again, the saga of the *Wagon Mound* and its ensuing litigation provides further evidence of how the common law often stumbles along with analytical hope as much as principled conviction. Never settled or certain, it lends itself to fresh interpretations as social mores and expectations change. Of course, this is no guarantee that the courts will always strike the right or appropriate balance. But it does ensure that the common law functions as a vibrant, not moribund process. Like so much else, the common law is ours and is only as persuasive or compelling as our own sense of justice.

4

THE POLITICS OF LAW

Cats, pigeons and old chestnuts

Lawyers and judges spend a lot of time insisting that 'law' stands to the side and apart from politics. While it is conceded that there are obvious connections and interactions between the two, it is an article of jurisprudential faith that judicial decision making continues on its own terms; it is largely carried out in a professional and detached manner. Judges appreciate the political origins and consequences of their decisions, but they resist the allegation that their own work and contribution are tainted by partisan bias or ideological commitments. If there is a resort to political views and material interests, it is made neutrally and objectively. Indeed, the power and legitimacy of adjudication in a democratic state seem to depend on some account of law being separate from politics. Like referees and umpires, judges are in the politics game, but not players or protagonists in its performance.

Of course, there are many who do not buy this image. For them, its defence is itself a posture of self-serving political convenience; it is all smoke and mirrors. Instead, it is argued that judges and lawyers' efforts to carve off their professional bailiwick from that of their political cousins is both unconvincing and wrong-headed. Viewed from a critical perspective, the common law is more accurately and usefully portrayed, like Clausewitz's understanding of war, as a continuing process of politics by other means. While judges (and lawyers) talk in a rarefied accent and specialized argot, they are still speaking and trading in the language of politics. This is not to suggest that judges are involved in a Machiavellian conspiracy or something equally suspect; they almost all fulfil their duties in good faith. However, wishing something to be true (i.e., that law is not politics) does not make it so – law and politics are inextricably mixed in with each other. And the effort to insist otherwise is of the most starkly political kind.

One of the most famous and arguably greatest cases in law is the American case *Marbury v. Madison* in 1803. Referred to as the 'fountainhead of judicial review', it is the decision which determined that courts are the final arbiters of what the American Constitution does and does not demand of the other branches of government. As the political satirist P. J. O'Rourke characteristically phrased it, it is more or less obligatory to cite *Marbury* when before the Supreme Court of the United States because 'it's like telling your wife her dress looks pretty before you go to a party'. However, as influential as it is, the case drives home the almost inevitable if contested connections between law and politics. The characters involved and the circumstances in which it occurred underline the pervasive interaction between the worlds of law and politics. There are as many who point to *Marbury* as exhibit number one in arguing for the separation of law and politic as there are those who protest that it demonstrates exactly the opposite. The fact that the decision remains pertinent and important today over 200 years after its rendering is testament to its ongoing vital and controversial stature in the common law canon of constitutional cases.

A POLITICAL THICKET

Politics in the early decades of the American Republic were as political and cut-throat as they come. A relatively small nation of 4 million people looking for a unique national identity after its revolutionary break from the United Kingdom, the United States was governed by an elite group of men who often used their grand and honourable ambitions as something of a cover for more prosaic concerns. In their efforts to forge a 'City upon a Hill', they fell prey to petty and personal politics. Even as they sought to build a democracy worthy of its name, some of its leading lights – George Washington, John Adams, Thomas Jefferson, Alexander Hamilton, James Madison, and the like – were more intent on settling old scores and making parochial political gains, especially when old friends became new enemies. It was a time for sharp wits and thick skin: the romantic drama of nation building often belied the mean squabbles of its ego-fragile builders. Although *Marbury v. Madison* was framed and subsequently celebrated in the highest legal and formal terms, it was set against and amidst the most basic of political wranglings: the urge to secure power for friends and to disempower enemies. The language may have been high constitutional principle, but the motivations were of a much grubbier kind.

At the end of the eighteenth century, the Democratic–Republican rivalry had not yet come to dominate American politics. Rather, the fundamental tension was between the Federalists (who campaigned under Hamilton and Adams for a strong central and national government) and the Antifederalists (who, led by Jefferson and Madison, favoured a more decentralised scheme of states' rights and powers). This cast of strong characters played out a long-running political drama that captivated the nation as they fought to control the thrust and import of the United States' 1789 Constitution. Although this engagement made its way to the Supreme Court, it did not end there. On the surface, the *Marbury* case involved the rather mundane issue of whether a justice of the peace could push through his delayed appointment. But its political context and immediate effects were distinctly more profound and widespread. It was only many decades later that the larger institutional impact of the decision was felt. And, it can be added, it is still being felt today.

In 1789, George Washington became the first President of the United States. With political courage and savvy, he was keen to appoint to his cabinet persons from all shades of the political spectrum. In particular, he made the Federalist

Alexander Hamilton his Treasury Secretary and the Antifederalist Thomas Jefferson his Secretary of State. For a short period, this made for a more stable and efficacious political culture. However, by 1796, any pretence at political harmony and bipartisan cooperation had dissipated. With the Federalist John Adams elected President and Jefferson as Vice President (under a soon-to-be-repealed Constitutional provision that made the election runner-up Vice President), the Federalist/Antifederalist contretemps was in full force and effect. Hamilton (joined by John Adams) and Jefferson (joined by James Madison) were on opposite sides of the political fence. By the time of the next election in late 1800, the political divisions were deep and divisive.

If Adams and Hamilton were the Federalist champions of republican government, then Jefferson was their Antifederalist doppelganger. Born to an elite Virginia slave-owning family in 1743, Thomas Jefferson was a lawyer and statesman supreme; he was to hold all the country's highest offices, including that of President from 1801 to 1809. Throughout his career, he championed state power over federal authority; he maintained that each branch of government should be able to decide for itself whether a law was constitutional within its own jurisdictional sphere. Although Jefferson and Marshall were cousins and Founding Fathers in the 1780s, there was little love lost between them. Indeed, by 1801, it can fairly be said that they had come to detest each other. Feuding in public, the two were openly hostile and were not above personal and political name calling. In short, the litigation in *Marbury v. Madison* in 1803 was one more site for the continuing, if stylized, bouts of mud-slinging, political one-upmanship and plain ugliness that marked and marred their relationship.

After losing the presidential election in November 1800 to Jefferson, Adams was entitled to remain in office until March 1801. During this novel 'lame duck' period, Adams made the fateful decision to make life as difficult as possible for his successor. Adams and his Federalist supporters passed the *District of Columbia Organic Act of 1801* and the *Judiciary Act of 1801*. These had the effect of allowing the President to increase the number of federal courts and to staff them with new judicial appointments. Commonly labelled 'the midnight judges', the appointments were largely pro-Federalist; the vast bulk of the sixteen federal judges and forty-two justices of the peace nominated were enthusiastic Adams supporters and, as importantly, strong political opponents of Jefferson.

However, in a situation that today would be seen as wildly conflicted and hugely improper, Adams had also appointed John Marshall to be the new Chief Justice of the Supreme Court; he later boasted that 'my gift of John Marshall to the people of the United States was the proudest act of my life'. When Marshall took judicial office at the end of January 1801, he remained in his previous post as Secretary of State until Jefferson took office. A seasoned statesman in his own right, he was tasked with putting into effect Adams's judicial appointments. After being approved by the Senate, this involved physically delivering the commissions to the new judges. While he managed to complete the formalities of most of these judicial appointments, there were still four remaining when Jefferson became President and Marshall ceased to be Secretary of State.

One of those incomplete commissions was that of William Marbury Jr. At the age of 38, he had been nominated for the post of Justice of the Peace in the District of Columbia. This was a powerful position that would have given him a legislative role and also made him the chief law enforcement officer for taxes, slaves and general criminal offenses. It had been held previously by Washington, Jefferson and Madison, so it carried a certain prestige as well as power. Unlike other federal judgeships, it did not require legal training. Being a gift of political patronage, this was an ideal role for someone of Marbury's background and ambitions.

William Marbury Jr. was grandson of a Maryland land-owner. A lifelong Federalist of the Adams camp, he began as a clerk to Maryland's auditor-general and became the Agent for the State; this was the State's most powerful unelected official and, being responsible for collecting debts and back taxes, enabled him to make many advantageous side deals. After

FIGURE 4.1. William Marbury Jr. James Madison
University Archives

his father frittered away his inheritance, William had made his
own fortune by finagling his political connections to speculate
in state-backed securities; he also became a shareholder and
director in a very successful bank. A close associate of President Adams, he lobbied actively against Jefferson in the tie-
breaking vote in the presidential election of 1800. His reward
was his appointment as a Justice of the Peace. If his commission was formally approved, William would have redeemed
the family name and set himself on course for further political
success.

After all these bureaucratic machinations and with several
personal vendettas in play, the stage was set for a political
donnybrook of the first order. Ironically, when Jefferson
finally took the reins of power on 4 March 1801, he was
sworn into office by Chief Justice Marshall. Jefferson would
be faced not only by a federal judiciary that was stacked with
political opponents but also that the head of that powerful
group would be one of Adams's closest confidantes, John

Marshall. This was not an appetizing prospect. But Jefferson was determined to manage and turn the situation to his own advantage. In fact, he set about precipitating a constitutional crisis that would encompass and perhaps resolve several pressing tensions. Primary among these was the issue of who got the final power to declare laws and official acts unconstitutional (as there was no clause in the Constitution about the interpretation and enforcement of the Constitution): was it the executive or judicial branch of government? And, if it was the executive branch, which level of government, federal or state, could exercise that power? The cards were dealt and the stakes were high.

PRESIDENTS AND COURTS

One of Jefferson's first acts of presidential office was to repeal the *Judiciary Act of 1801* and put the circuit court responsibilities back with the Supreme Court. Although the Supreme Court justices were still Federalists for the most part, the Antifederalists could at least appoint more of their own as there was no clause in the Constitution about the interpretation and enforcement of the Constitution, as years went on. Partly out of caution and partly for sheer retribution, the government also suspended the 1802 Supreme Court sitting to let things calm down and perhaps win more seats in the 1802 midterm elections. Most pertinently, an emboldened Jefferson had instructed his new Secretary of State, Levi Lincoln, not to deliver the outstanding commissions, including Marbury's.

In December 1801, a frustrated Marbury filed his legal petition for executive action on his commission directly to the Supreme Court. He argued that the foundational *Judiciary Act of 1789* gave the Supreme Court original jurisdiction over various petitions and orders, not merely appellate involvement. Accordingly, he sought a direct court order compelling President Jefferson's then Secretary of State, James Madison, to deliver his commission: this was known as a *writ of mandamus* (i.e., a judicial order compelling the commissions to be delivered). Of course, Madison himself was no slouch in the

FIGURE 4.2. James Madison. The White House Historical
Association, www.whitehousehistory.org/.

political arena: he was also a Founding Father and he would
become the fourth President of the United States in 1809. He
was also no friend of the new Chief Justice. He publicly
excoriated Marshall as a tool of Virginia's financial specula-
tors and a recipient of favours from the Bank of the United
States. Such charges were known to and declared 'malignant'
by Chief Justice Marshall.

However, it was Jefferson who was calling the government
shots. It was his wager that the Supreme Court would recognize that certain acts of the executive were outside its jurisdiction. Failing that, he gambled that even if this did not occur,
the Supreme Court would be unable to enforce any orders that
it made against the executive; this would diminish the future
power and role of the federal courts. However, Jefferson did
not count on the political and jurisprudential nous of John
Marshall.

Initially, the Supreme Court asked Madison to show cause
as to why the Supreme Court should not issue such an order.
In a singular act of political brinkmanship, Jefferson insisted

that Madison should ignore the order and that the government should thumb their collective noses at the Supreme Court. Also, Jefferson orchestrated a denouncement in Congress by John Randolph of Virginia (one of his cousins) of the Supreme Court's 'inquisitorial capacity'.

This left the Supreme Court with little option other than to address the matter head on. In order to do so, the Supreme Court had to address three separate and related questions:

(1) Did Article III of the Constitution ('In all cases affecting Ambassadors, other public ministers and consuls, and those in which a state shall be a party, the Supreme Court shall have original jurisdiction, ... [but] in all other cases shall have appellate jurisdiction') offer an exhaustive list of powers or could it be supplemented by Congress?

(2) If Congress did attempt to modify the Constitution by the *Judiciary Act of 1789* ('the Supreme Court ... shall have power to issue ... writs of mandamus'), is it the Constitution or Congress that prevails?

(3) Which institution – the Supreme Court, the Executive, or Congress – has the ultimate authority to resolve such matters?

After a short hearing in early February 1803, the Supreme Court delivered its judgment a very short time later on 24 February. It was a unanimous decision written by Chief Justice Marshall. Considering that the bench was far from sympathetic to Jefferson's government (as they were each appointed by Presidents Washington or Adams), this was no mean feat in itself. Indeed, it testifies to both the judges' sensitivity to maintaining the appearance of political neutrality and to Marshall's political skills at effecting a compromise among the strong and occasionally antagonistic members of the Supreme Court – Samuel Chase (who had been unsuccessfully impeached by Jefferson's Congress and was a business adversary of Marbury); Alfred Moore (who was an Adams loyalist); William Cushing (who had known Federalist leanings); William Paterson (a long-serving senator and state attorney-general); and Bushrod Washington (who was Washington's nephew and was appointed by Adams). As things turned out, neither Cushing nor Moore participated in the case as they were ill.

The decision and reasoning of the Supreme Court is very technical and obscure; it only comes to life when read and understood against the political shenanigans behind it. In an impressive act of political high-wire acrobatics, the Supreme Court struck a posture that was subtle and nuanced in both reasoning and result – Marbury had the right to his com- mission, but the Supreme Court did not have jurisdiction to enforce that right because Congress unconstitutionally expanded the power of the Supreme Court in the *Judiciary Act of 1789*. In short, the *Marbury* decision let Jefferson off the political hook, but only at the cost of accepting that the courts trumped the executive on constitutional interpretation.

In reaching and defending this stance, Chief Justice Marshall tackled the questions raised by Marbury's petition in a three-stage process. First, he determined that Marbury had the right to the commission he demanded; he was legally appointed by the President in accordance with the *Judiciary Act of 1801* and was, therefore, entitled to the 'property' and benefits of the office for the statutory term of five years.

Secondly, Marshall went on to determine if there was a remedy for the violation of that right. As the United States was 'a government of laws, and not men', he observed that 'it will certainly cease to deserve this high appellation if the laws furnish no remedy for the violation of a vested legal right'. Accordingly, Marshall insisted that there must be a remedy available for the violation of legal right. In doing so, Marshall makes an important distinction between those executive acts that are reviewable (i.e., those of a distinctly political character, such as who to appoint to judicial office) and those that are not (i.e., once appointed, the person had a vested legal right that was open to scrutiny and enforcement through the courts). As he put it, while exercises of executive discretion 'are only politically examinable ... where a specific duty is assigned by law, and individual rights depend upon the performance of that duty ... the individual who considers himself injured has a right to resort to the laws of his country for a remedy'.

Thirdly, Marshall had to apply this reasoning to the facts of Marbury's case and decide if he was entitled to the particular remedy, a writ of mandamus, for which he applied. In a crucial move, he breaks this crucial question into two separate issues: what was the nature of the writ applied for; and whether the Supreme Court could issue such writs. By making this differentiation, Marshall managed to steer the discussion into the underlying and motivating matter that put Jefferson and Marshall at loggerheads – whether Congress's *Judiciary Act of 1789* conflicted with the Constitution and, if so, whether the Supreme Court could strike down and invalidate it. Of course, there is really no deeper or more broad-ranging determination than that; its resolution would set the political and constitutional stage for generations to come.

After some important historical digressions about British jurisprudence, Marshall reached the relatively uncontroversial conclusion that this is a 'plain case of mandamus'. He then moved on to the real kicker, which is whether the granting of such power to the Supreme Court under the *Judiciary Act of 1789* is permitted by Article III of the Constitution: 'if this Court is not authorized to issue a writ of mandamus to such an officer, it must be because the law is unconstitutional and therefore absolutely incapable of conferring the authority and assigning the duties which its words purport to confer and assign'. In a bold and far-reaching argument, Marshall found that the 1789 act conflicts with the Constitution because it seeks to give original jurisdiction to the Supreme Court in areas where the Constitution only confers appellate jurisdiction (except under very specific circumstances that did not apply in Marbury's case). It was not the case, as Marbury had argued, that Article III only established a 'floor' that could be added to or modified by Congress: 'to what purpose are powers limited . . . if these limits may, at any time, be passed by those intended to be restrained'. If Congress had power to vary the constitution, then Marshall noted that its effect would be 'form without substance' and render the constitution of little fundamental force.

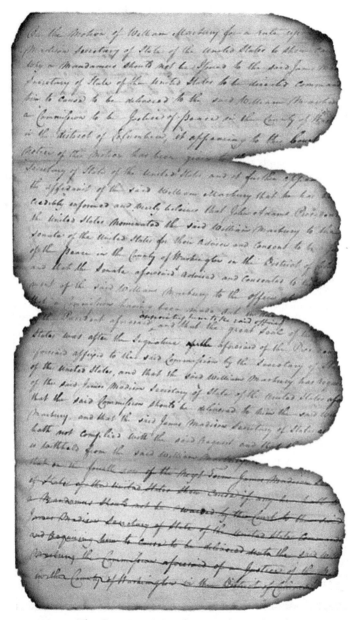

FIGURE 4.3. The Court's opinion, bearing the marks of the Capitol fire of 1898. National Archives and Records Administration, www.archives.gov/exhibits/charters/charters_of_freedom_ zoom_pages/charters_of_freedom_zoom_8.1.1.html.

In one fell swoop, Marshall not only offered a differing interpretation of the Constitution to that offered by Jefferson's government and also Marbury, but also asserted the power of the Supreme Court to prevail in such a constitutional face-off. In words that ring resonantly and strongly even today, Marshall sought to ground the political and constitutional basis of judicial review:

So if a law be in opposition to the constitution: if both the law and the constitution apply to a particular case, so that the court must either decide that case conformably to the law, disregarding the constitution; or conformably to the constitution, disregarding the law: the court must determine which of these conflicting rules governs the case. This is of the very essence of judicial duty.

If then the courts are to regard the constitution; and the constitution is superior to any ordinary act of the legislature; the constitution, and not such ordinary act, must govern the case to which they both apply.

Those then who controvert the principle that the constitution is to be considered, in court, as a paramount law, are reduced to the necessity of maintaining that courts must close their eyes on the constitution, and see only the law. This doctrine would subvert the very foundation of all written constitutions.

TWO HUNDRED YEARS AFTER

Of course, no decision automatically becomes a great or important case simply from the virtue of being made. It needs to be accepted by both the legal and popular community as being compelling and appropriate. This is particularly so with a case of *Marbury*'s significance and import; it had the potential to be a game changer and influence matters of a much broader and sweeping nature than the particular issue in dispute. While it is now clear that the principles established in *Marbury* have had a seismic effect on American (and other common law jurisdictions') constitutional law and politics, the attainment of that stature has been neither swift nor uncontroversial.

The immediate response to *Marbury* was muted and unexceptional. There was no recorded discussion in Congress.

Contemporary newspapers published the decision in full, but reserved their editorials for comments entirely in terms of its political effect on the President's power and the continuing set – to between Federalists and Antifederalists – Jefferson had prevailed but received a public scolding for his troubles. Although there was much debate about whether the Supreme Court and Marshall personally had gone too far in chastising the President, the larger principle of judicial review was by and large ignored. Indeed, Marshall never struck down another act of Congress in his long tenure as Chief Justice. However, as the decades passed, the focus of constitutional scrutiny shifted from presidential powers to the courts' ultimate authority to control the meaning and enforcement of the Constitution. It is not so much the *Marbury* judgment itself that binds, but the principle that others have wanted to see in it and entrench as constitutional gospel.

Throughout the nineteenth century, *Marbury* was viewed as a case about the mandamus and original jurisdiction. At its most expansive, it was viewed as about the balance of power between the different branches of government. The Supreme Court was seen to be fulfilling a traditional common law as a check on the extravagant exercise of untrammelled power by the Executive and Legislative branches; it was a vital part of the Montesquieian checks and balances on which the American Constitution was supposedly based. Indeed, four years after *Marbury* in *United States v. Burr*, the main issue was whether the Supreme Court could compel the President to disclose evidence held by the executive branch; the Court held that it could. Yet, in an era when a strong version of individual rights enforcement had not fully inserted itself into American jurisprudence, the role of the courts was largely confined to a supervisory and reactive role in constitutional politics.

However, at the beginning of the twentieth century, the importance of *Marbury*'s assertion of judicial supremacy began to take hold. Courts began to flex their muscles and place much tighter controls on government power and actions. Not surprisingly, there developed a corresponding critique of its validity and worth. Now framed as 'the counter-majoritarian difficulty', it was contended that unelected judges had no democratic basis or legitimacy for imposing or elevating their views of the Constitution's meaning over those of the nation's elected representatives. Moreover, there was no political basis for the courts to supplement and read into the Constitution rights and principles that were not immediately obvious on its face or in the historical record. This objection became even more practical and insistent as the politics of the Supreme Court began to diverge more significantly from those of the nation's legislatures and popular views.

This all came to a head in the infamous decision of *Lochner* in 1905. It involved early attempts to introduce pro-worker legislation that limited the number of hours that could be worked each day and per week. In a 5–4 decision, the Supreme Court held that, far from protecting the working conditions and health of workers, the legislation infringed on the 14th Amendment's guarantee that no state 'shall deprive any person of life, liberty, or property without due process of law'. By regulating the terms on which people could be employed, the legislation was an 'unreasonable, unnecessary, and arbitrary interference with the right and liberty of the individual to contract'. By so deciding, the Supreme Court placed itself and *Marbury*'s principle and practice of judicial review directly in the eye of the political storm where it has remained ever since. Yet, for all the criticism heaped upon particular court decisions, the Supreme Court itself has managed to weather the storms and retain a certain constitutional legitimacy.

Although there have been ups and downs in the Supreme Court's exercise of its activist authority, the basic principle of judicial supremacy – that courts can invalidate legislation on whatever constitutional basis its judges consider appealing or acceptable – is now no longer debatable. The key question is how the Supreme Court should go about exercising that breathtaking power and institutional responsibility. Although the theoretical and scholarly battle is waged around jurisprudential theories of constitutional interpretation (formalist, originalist, pragmatist, progressive, etc.), the underlying tension remains political. Both judges and commentators tend to support as valid and legitimate those decisions that they favour politically and to criticize those that they do not. Abortion, health care, gay marriage, police powers, schooling and the like are now squarely within the jurisdictional mandate of the Supreme Court; the final word is with the judges, not the politicians. If *Marbury* sowed the wind of judicial democracy, then modern society has reaped the whirlwind of judocracy.

In many ways, the institution of judicial review has fared better in other common law countries and the rest of the world. The tendency has been to grant courts the power to interpret the Constitution but to allow legislatures a more even-handed opportunity to respond to and even reject judicial decisions about the constitutionality of particular legislative acts or executive actions. Canada is a good example of this tendency. Historically, the courts have adopted a more deferential stance towards the other branches of government and have seen themselves as being partners in a dialogue about constitutional meaning and demands. However, in more modern constitutional amendments, the other branches of government are given the constitutional power to exempt legislation from constitutional review. While this possibility has important symbolic and institutional significance, it has been infrequently used. Consequently, it is a more modest and less expansive version of *Marbury* that has been incorporated by other legal systems, like Canada, into their constitutional arrangements.

What the legacy of *Marbury* has done is to oblige people to address and determine how democracy is best served and advanced. Some contend that it is by a governmental scheme of direct democracy in which the people themselves or their elected agents decide what is best for society. Others insist that it is by a constitutional arrangement that places court-enforced constraints in the name of a more substantive vision of democracy on what the people or their elected agents can do. This, of course, is itself the most highly charged and ideological of issues. As such, *Marbury* and its progeny have put the judicial cats firmly among the political pigeons. Indeed, many today remain confused about exactly who the cats are and who the pigeons are.

HISTORY'S VERDICT

For all the fuss and bother generated by the prelude to the *Marbury* decision and its continuing constitutional significance, the political fall-out from the Supreme Court's judgment was relatively contained. All the major players went on their merry way and managed to confirm their status as founding members of the select pantheon of American greats – Marshall went on to become the longest serving (thirty-four years) and probably most esteemed Chief Justice of the American tradition; Madison became the fourth President of the United States from 1809 to 1817; Jefferson continued as President until 1809 and is still considered to be one of the most effective presidents in American history; and Alexander Hamilton was killed in a duel with Aaron Burr, the sitting Vice President, in July 1804. Marshall and Jefferson continued their personal and political spat for many years; both supported publications that freely criticized the other and they were not above the occasional private condemnation of the other as 'hypocritical' and 'immoral'.

All did well, except for Marbury. Like so many litigants before him, William Marbury is the forgotten man of his eponymous litigation. For all his struggles, he never did get his judicial appointment. Although the Supreme Court declared that he had a right to his commission, it decided that it did not have the jurisdiction to enforce that right against the executive branch of government. This effectively stymied Marbury's political ambitions. However, he did continue to lead a very successful business career; he became the first purchasing agent for the Washington Navy Yard and a Director of the Bank of Columbia and Potomac Canal Company. Indeed, as a wealthy man, he purchased in December 1800 a grand house overlooking the Potomac River in Washington. The house still stands today and is home to the Ukrainian Embassy. Further, in the 1980s, Marbury's portrait was hung by Chief Justice Warren Burger in the John Marshall Room at the Supreme Court, along with James Madison's. Marbury might well have felt that the success and affirmation that had eluded him in the aftermath of the Supreme Court's was granted by posterity.

5

THE COMPANIES WE KEEP

The moralities of business

'A good reputation is more valuable than money'.

Publilius Syrus

Trade and commerce are as old as society itself. People have bartered and sought to enrich themselves for millennia. In seeking ever more efficient and profitable ways to do that, various schemes and structures have been imaginatively devised. The most common initiative has been for traders and entrepreneurs to band together in partnerships in the hope of obtaining a collective advantage. However, the idea of a 'corporation' as we know it today was a long time coming. The corporation has its roots in Roman law (and is derivative of the Latin *corporare* for 'form into a body') and the state-sponsored colonial organisations of the seventeenth century, like The East India Company and The Hudson's Bay Company. But the recognition of a collective entity or institution that warranted a distinct identity and legal *persona* independent of its participating members is of relatively recent origin.

In the British Commonwealth, the nineteenth century English case of *Salomon* is considered to have cemented the place of the modern corporation at the centre of today's social and commercial life. Somewhat incongruously, this celebrated precedent begins in the filthy backstreets of Dickensian London where the Salomon family struggled to keep its boot-making business afloat. From these decidedly humble and dubious beginnings, the laws of corporate governance have developed to facilitate the immense growth and influential presence of today's megacorporations. Much has been attributed to the *Salomon* decision's important role in establishing the identity of the corporation as a legal entity separate from its (founding) owners and imposing a veil between the corporation and its shareholders.

Yet, upon closer inspection, the whole *Salomon* saga is revealed to be about much less and much more. It is more helpfully understood as a decision that is less about the legal consequences of incorporation and more about the morality of business practices. How do we handle the keeping of moral obligations to others when doing so will result in catastrophic consequences for ourselves? Consequently, in revisiting the case of *Salomon*, it is illuminating to tackle the more broader and more ambitious question of the vexing relationship between legal principles and moral obligations in a commercial world. Taking a cue from Ambrose Bierce, it might be asked whether the corporation is merely 'an ingenious device for obtaining profit without individual responsibility' or whether it can be appreciated as something in which individual responsibility and profit making can be combined.

A FOUL DRAIN

Whitechapel in the East End of London is still a hubbub of commercial enterprise; it is as marked by its ethnic diversity as it is by its commercial ingenuity. But, later in the nineteenth century, it was also a site of devastating poverty and dire squalor. If the old saw of 'where there's muck, there's money' has any truth to it, then Whitechapel was a very rich place. For all its industrial wealth, it was more a cesspit than a Silicon Valley; it brimmed with breweries, tanneries, sweatshops, and abattoirs. The streets stunk with all manner of industrial effluence and moral decay; drunkards, prostitutes and urchins mingled with traders, entrepreneurs and Salvationists. Alexis de Tocqueville's words very much hit the mark: 'From this

FIGURE 5.1. Whitechapel High Street, 1880s.

foul drain the greatest stream of human industry flows out to fertilize the whole world. Here humanity attains its most complete development and its most brutish, here civilisation works its miracles and civilised man is turned almost into a savage'.

At this time, Whitechapel and a cast of local characters fed off each other. The gruesome murders of Jack the Ripper baffled the authorities and plagued the nightmares of local denizens; the carnivalesque exploitation of Joseph 'Elephant Man' Merrick captured public attention; and the socialist beginnings of George Bernard Shaw and the Fabians and revolutionary education of the exiled Vladimir Ilyich Ulyanov ('Lenin') were fostered. It was a time of great historical consequence, but for many in Whitechapel the constant grind of daily life muted the excitement.

One unheralded member of these East Enders was Aron Salomon. He was a young man in his early twenties when he arrived in this latter-day Gomorrah in about 1860 from Velbert in Prussia (near today's Dusseldorf). An orthodox Jew, he soon became part of the strong religious neighbourhood in Whitechapel and married a local girl, Schoontje. Around this time, Jews were no longer encumbered with any particular legal or formal prohibitions on carrying out business or participating in the community; the first Jewish Lord Mayor of London, David Salomons, was elected in 1855 and Lionel de Rothschild was permitted to take his elected seat in Parliament in 1858 when the oath of office was amended to include non-Christians. Nevertheless, there was still a strong current of anti-Semitism in London that pervaded the business and legal elite. Aron Salomon was frequently caricatured as the stereotypical 'grasping merchant'.

Aron set about establishing himself in his personal and commercial life. Both went well. He began to operate as a boot and leather merchant. By 1862, his first child, Emanuel, was born. Adding to the family at regular intervals, there was a brood of six children, five boys and a girl, by the mid-1870s. The firm also thrived and Aron was able to bring his sons into the business as they grew up. As testament to his improved standing in the local business community, Aron was able to obtain the sponsorship of four local worthies and became a naturalized citizen in 1873. Buoyed by government contracts, Salomon & Sons was now a reputed boot and leather merchant. It had become a fixture of Whitechapel High Street; they were no fly-by-night operation.

Over the next twenty years or so, Salomon's business went from strength to strength. Under the managerial initiative of Aron and his sons, it expanded to Northampton, the traditional centre of England's leather industry. Rather than trade under the Salomon name alone, the family developed a couple of local firms, Fitzwell and Davy Brothers. The precise inter-relationships of the family-owned group is unclear, but later suspicions of surreptitious money-shuffling complicated later controversies around the Salomons. However, by the 1890s, the family-named business alone was valued at over £10,000 (well over $1 million in today's money).

The Salomons prided themselves on making high-quality products. In 1890, the firm won the highest award for their military apparel at the Royal Military Exhibition in Chelsea. Moreover, in an age that was notorious for 'sweat labour', the Salomon enterprises, while not without flaws or failings, stood somewhat apart from other exploitative employers in the leather trade. As devout Jews (and active in local synagogues), they made a practice of philanthropic giving to alleviate the tribulations of local indigents. Indeed, when another manufacturer was chosen to supply the East End Jewish Boot Fund, Aron wrote to the *Jewish Chronicle* to complain that, if he had been invited to tender for the role, he would have provided a superior product at cost price. Consequently, although the family was no friend at all to the nascent trade-union movement, Salomon & Sons could claim a sincere commitment to being an honourable and respected employer and merchant of its day. The Salomons were not just a business in the eyes of their peers; they were accepted and active members in a *community*.

In early 1892, Aron decided to incorporate the business and obtain the benefits of limited liability. Aron was scrupulous in following the formal and artificial requirements of the *Companies Act 1862* to the letter. The law required documentation of ostensible 'transactions' (between, effectively, Salomon and himself) where no funds ever changed hands and exchanges of value were of the most intangible variety. However, regardless of the legal ramifications of taking this step, the more pressing and immediate concern was with the moral quality of such a manoeuvre – did he do it to steal a march on his creditors? Was it to protect members of his family from claims against their future well-being? Was it to simply join a trend of incorporation that was becoming more common among small business? Was it a matter of commercial gain getting the better of his communal obligations?

Aron began by arranging a trustee, Adolph Anholt, for the future company and entering into an agreement with him for the company's purchase of the business from Aron. For these purposes, the business was valued at a modest £40,000. As the *Companies Act 1862* required that a corporation have at least seven shareholders, Aron, his wife, and five of his children signed the memorandum of incorporation, each taking a £1 share. By way of compensation, Aron received £1,000 cash, was granted 20,000 shares of the new company (which meant he held 20,001 of the 20,007 shares issued), and was approved for 100 £100 debentures for a total of £10,000. Of course, the reality was that, as Salomon himself was the driving force behind the purchase of his own firm, the £1,000 cash transfer was from himself to himself. Additionally, the remaining nearly £8,000 of what was ultimately a £39,000 purchase price was paid to Salomon in the form of pre-existing debt fulfilment. In effect, any cash consideration owed to Salomon by the new corporation was satisfied by discharging the original Salomon firm's old debts to Aron (which were eventually repaid in full).

The company was registered as 'A. Salomon & Co. Ltd.' and came into existence on 28 July 1892: Aron was appointed managing director and two of his sons, Emanuel and Salomon, became directors. The first meeting of the shareholders was held a few days later on 2 August 1892. All the financial arrangements between Aron and the company were settled by the end of January 1893. Little else changed; the business was still entirely family-owned and run. But it was at this point that things began to unravel.

With a general downturn in the economy, labour disruption and the loss of some government contracts, Salomon & Co. began to feel the squeeze; unsold stock was accumulating and earnings were down. Exactly whether Aron saw this coming assumes huge significance in the moral and legal facts of the matter. There is certainly no evidence that the incorporation was an obvious first step in a larger fraudulent scheme to avoid creditors or accrue some speculative profit; Aron was not involved in an unmitigated swindle. Importantly, all pre-incorporation debts were paid in full. But there were clouds of ethical suspicion that swirled around the transaction, especially when it came time for Aron to take legal advantage of his manoeuvre. The most reasonable assumption seems to be that there were several factors (e.g., a desire for a more formal role for his children and for greater respectability) combined with a general foreboding about a range of economic pressures on Salomon & Co. As with most such episodes, neither motivations nor intentions were entirely transparent.

E. F. Broderip, J.P.

FIGURE 5.2. Edmund Broderip. Courtesy of Bath Royal Literary
and Scientific Institute.

On 5 February 1893, in order to tide the struggling
company over, Aron secured a £5,000 personal loan from
Edmund Broderip, another local merchant. Aron then loaned
this amount to the company at a 10 per cent annual interest.
As security for the loan, Aron mortgaged his debentures
(valued at £10,000) to Broderip. Unfortunately, the business
deteriorated precipitously. In September, the company
defaulted on the interest payments to Broderip. As was his

entitlement, Broderip indicated that he would call in the loan principal. A month later on 11 October, when he had not received further payment, Broderip commenced an action to enforce his security. On 25 October 1893, A. Salomon & Co. Ltd. officially went into receivership. The business was ending, but the legal fun and games were just beginning.

THE COMPANY IS BORN

Now under the control of the receiver, Salomon & Co. contested Broderip's claim to the principal on the debentures. If Broderip's claim were satisfied (which it eventually was), it would exhaust almost all the remaining assets of the company; only slightly more than £1,000 would remain to satisfy the other creditors' claims of over £7,500. But, perhaps more significantly, the receiver also brought an accompanying action against Aron Salomon himself. It was alleged that the creation of Salomon & Co. was a sham, an elaborate and fraudulent scheme perpetrated by Aron to defeat the legitimate claims of the company's creditors. As such, the receiver insisted that the company's formation should be set aside and Aron made personally responsible for the company's debts. In short, he was being asked to give up his debentures as well as repay to the company the almost £30,000 that he had received on the company's formation.

Aron not only did not have such funds (well over $3 million in today's money), but continued to insist that he had not acted inappropriately, let alone fraudulently. As such, he not only resisted the receiver's claim but also maintained that, as a debenture-holder, he had his own claims against the company that outranked other trade creditors. This obduracy did not impress the business community and also brought into doubt Aron's original motives for incorporating his family business. In slightly condescending and anti-Semitic terms, the *Shoe and Leather Record* opined that Aron should cease to engage in 'financial juggling with a vengeance' that placed in jeopardy his 'unblemished reputation . . . as one of the best men in the Jewish community'. His attempt to enforce his strictly legal entitlements was characterised as resulting from 'evil counsels'. Undeterred, Aron continued to insist that he had done nothing wrong. He hired Ralph Raphael as his solicitor and set about defending his money and his family's honour.

The scene was nicely set to determine whether Aron was acting fairly and, if not, what should be his comeuppance. However, although this ethical issue was at the heart of the dispute, the lawyers framed the matter in more strictly legal terms. Instead of addressing the moral issue of 'fair dealing' directly, they were successful in persuading the courts to characterise it as being about the nature and extent, if any, of the separation between a company and its founding and directing personalities. If there was a true separation, then Aron was free and clear; if not, then Aron was on the hook for Broderip's and other creditors' claims.

A close reading of the various judgments in *Salomon* strongly recommends that the case was less about corporate personality in itself and more about whether its benefits accrue to those whose motivations for effecting incorporation were dubious at best. After all, the principle of 'separate corporate personality' had already been in play in English company law for a half-century or so since the decision in *R v. Arnaud* in 1846. In general terms, therefore, the question was whether incorporators could be reprimanded by virtue of their failure to engage in 'fair dealing'. The stakes were high because, without an authoritative affirmation of the corporation's separate legal personhood, the growth of a more capitalised economy was on the line (for better and worse). The touted benefits of incorporation – continuing existence, transferable ownership, limited liability, fund-raising capacity, professional management and the like – all flow from such recognition. Nevertheless, *Salomon*'s contemporary significance was to be found in its response to an ethical inquiry – were the advantages of incorporation only available to those who could claim to be acting fairly and, excepting outright fraudsters, were they open to all and sundry? This was and is no small matter.

THE *Salomon* CRUCIBLE

The case first came before the Queen's Bench Division in early November 1894. The presiding judge was Roland Vaughan Williams. Appointed by Lord Halsbury for whom he had 'devilled' (i.e., acted as a junior barrister for in his early years), he went on to the Court of Appeal a few years after the *Salomon* case. His judicial reputation was of being something of a stickler for technical niceties, a defender of the common law's unstructured pragmatism, and a rather all-round eccentric figure. He had been an esteemed lawyer and an expert in commercial law; he was the author of *The Law and Practice of Bankruptcy*. Doing little to hide his well-known opposition to incorporation that he considered almost tantamount to fraudulent conversion at its core, it came as little surprise that his 1895 Valentine's Day judgment went against Aron.

Although Vaughan Williams found that there was no fraud on the creditors, he relied on the novel argument (suggested by him to the plaintiff's lawyers) that the company was acting as an agent for Aron and that he was, therefore, the responsible principal throughout. Aron was required to indemnify the company for all its debts and his debentures declared to be unenforceable. In larger terms, this meant that Vaughan Williams had refused to accept that Salomon & Co. was a separate legal entity for all practical business purposes; the veil of incorporation was pulled back with little ceremony or compunction.

In short order, Aron took his case to the Court of Appeal. Through his barrister, the established (and talented sportsman) Montague Muir Mackenzie, it was contended that Aron had acted entirely in accordance with the letter and underlying policy of the *Companies Act*. The appeal was heard on 7 May 1895 and judgment was handed down on 28 May 1895. While all three judges rejected Vaughan Williams' line of reasoning, they still unanimously found against Salomon. The leading judgment was given by the prominent Lord Justice Lindley; he was already a reputed jurist and went on to become a leading law lord. He was hard on Aron and opined that the incorporation scheme was 'a device to defraud creditors' and 'not permitted by law'.

The other two took a similar line. Lord Justice Lopes characterised the other family members as 'six mere dummies' and concluded that 'to legalize such a transaction would be a scandal'. Lord Justice Kay was less scathing and would have allowed Aron to repay the full purchase price of the company, but with credit for the debentures (for which he had never received any money). The upshot was that companies like Salomon & Co. were a separate legal entity in name only – they did not shield its beneficial owners and continuing controllers from future liability, especially if there was a whiff of fraud about the initial incorporation.

For his part, Aron was now in a real bind. He had lost not only his company but also almost all of his money. The plight of impoverished persons in Whitechapel was not at all attractive. Not only was there grinding poverty on his doorstep, there was the unedifying prospect of the Poor House (a government-run workhouse). To say that Aron and his family might literally have been lining up for gruel and cleaning hospital refuse in exchange for filthy shelter would involve only little exaggeration. The Salomons would be down among the absolute dregs of a Dickensian society. So, with moral resolve and a little-else-to-lose mentality, an impecunious and dishonoured Aron made a successful bid to appeal to the House of Lords *in forma pauperis* (i.e., he was excused from paying legal fees if he lost). To do so, he had to swear that he had no funds or assets at all except £5 and the clothes that he was wearing.

The case was heard over three days in June 1896. Aron was represented by the heavyweight legal team of McCall, Buckley and Cohen QCs. Their basic argument was that, apart from compliance with all legislative requirements, the family business was in decent shape when incorporation occurred and that Aron had acted in good faith at all times. In response, the company's barristers, Farwell and Theobald, insisted that the whole incorporation was a scam and that Aron as the company's chief executive should be brought to personal account.

Six months later on 16 November 1896, the six judges of the House of Lords gave their opinions. In an abrupt and unanimous about-turn, they decided that there was nothing improper about Aron's actions, that the incorporation of A. Salomon & Co. Ltd. was entirely valid, and that Aron could hold on to whatever money that he still had. In effect, the House decided that, once the formalities of the *Companies Act 1862* had been followed, the incorporation of the company was complete and it amounted to a new entity separate from its founders and continuing owners. This was a resounding success for Aron and other similar family ventures. Henceforth, companies and their owners were not one and the same in law, no matter how identical they were in practice. Reinforcing a 'corporate veil' between the company and its members, the law lords confirmed that not only an association of businesspeople could become a truly chartered and freestanding corporation, but so could a one-person or family undertaking.

A strong opinion was delivered by Lord Halsbury. He was considered to be no great legal mind, but he exerted strong institutional influence through his political connections. As the Lord Chancellor (the country's chief law officer), he was also a member of the government's executive and legislative branch. Finding no provisions in the *Companies Act* about the need for a shareholder to be 'an independent and beneficially interested person', he saw nothing wrong with what Aron had done: 'Whether such a result be right or wrong, politic or impolitic, . . . we have nothing to do with . . . if this company has been duly constituted by law; and, whatever may be the motives of those whose who constitute it'. He was joined in this opinion by Lord Watson, Lord Herschell and the other law lords, Lords Morris and Davey.

Lord Macnaghten gave the most uncompromising and declaratory judgment. An Irishman and former Conservative MP, he was held in high regard by Bench and Bar alike; he had a wry turn of phrase and the ability to give the most technical arguments a stylish spin. And these qualities stood in him in good stead in this case. As much as he was ambivalent towards Aron's situation, he was persuaded that Aron had acted in good faith. He opined that the other creditors had been careless and 'have only themselves to blame for their misfortunes'. In a resounding statement of legal principle, he stated that:

> The company is at law a different person altogether from the sub-scribers to the memorandum; and, though it may be that after incorp-oration the business is precisely the same as it was before, and the same persons are managers, and the same hands receive the profits, the company is not in law the agent of the subscribers or trustee for them. Nor are the subscribers as members liable, in any shape or form, except to the extent and in the manner provided by the Act.

Salomon's decisive affirmation of a company's 'separate legal personality' was effected organically through the judge-made common law. As such, it demonstrated the serendipitous nature of the process as each court was unanimous, but in a different direction and/or with a different rationale. Neverthe-less, the ultimate decision reflected broadly the received under-standings of the time about the need to insulate capitalist speculation from managerial activity, even if both were embodied in one and the same person. This decision heralded the twentieth century and set the substance and tone for much of the 'corporate capitalism' that was to dominate the century.

BEHIND THE VEIL

For all its importance (or perhaps because of it), the *Salomon* decision was met with as much condemnation as praise. On the one hand, some worried about the ease with which the benefits of incorporation, particularly limited liability, could be obtained by all manner of small businesses or traders; it was now a relatively simple matter for families and one-person firms to shield their assets from legitimate creditors. This led to efforts to offer better protection to creditors by placing more onerous requirements (e.g., a debenture registry and increased regulatory oversights) on the formation of companies. On the other hand, some celebrated the fact that the benefits of incorporation were now more broadly available and would better grease the wheels of commerce at all levels; the decision rightly weakened the hand of creditors and obliged the more dubious among them to take greater responsibility for their often extortionate activities. Most significantly, Parliament stayed quiet and took no immediate steps to alter the thrust or effects of the law lords' robust decision. It was another example of the power of courts to develop and, on some interpretations, change legislative policy and practice. It was only in the 1900s that Parliament began to reassert itself and introduce important distinctions between so-called private and public corporations.

But perhaps the most telling effect was that *Salomon* was not treated as a decision about whether companies had separate legal identities as many modern accounts would have it. This outcome seems to have already been accepted by most lawyers and commentators; the law lords' decision simply acted as an authoritative confirmation of this principle. The more pressing and controversial result of *Salomon* was its effect of extending the benefits of incorporation to a much broader class of entrepreneurial ventures and, as importantly, detaching matters of legal correctness from ethical soundness. Henceforth, small and/or family businesses like Aron Salomon's which could not be viewed as genuinely associative entities (like the original joint-stock companies) were welcomed, albeit begrudgingly by some, into the broader community of corporate business. The decision spoke more concretely to the legitimacy of certain incorporations than to the fact that incorporation was not fraudulent in itself. However, it also brought into play an issue that continues to dominate company law today – what consequences follow from such a legal manoeuvre?

It has been the burden of company law to determine when and to what extent the fiction of the 'corporate veil' is to be preserved: when can it be pierced or peered behind? And by whom? Despite a century of efforts and suggestions, it would be fair to say that the courts have not managed to fashion or pursue a readily discernible set of operating principles. The only reliable observation is that there has been a marked reluctance on the part of judges to look behind the veil of incorporation except in the most flagrant instances of intentional wrongdoing: the corporation's separate personality is close to inviolate and treated as almost real. The durability of the corporate veil results from the robustness of neither the doctrine nor the fiction. It is rather an indicator that today, we think quite a lot of self-interested business dealings are fair. Importantly, the House of Lords in *Salomon* did not simply stop at declarations of black-letter law and judicial deference. Lord Macnaghten waded into the contestable waters of responsibility and fairness:

> The unsecured creditors of A. Salomon and Company, Limited, may be entitled to sympathy, but they have only themselves to blame for their misfortunes. They trusted the company, I suppose, because they had long dealt with Mr. Salomon, and he had always paid his way; but they had full notice that they were no longer dealing with an individual, and they must be taken to have been cognisant of the memorandum and of the articles of association.

As the legal validity of the incorporation was the very thing that Salomon's unsecured creditors were challenging, it is somewhat harsh to suggest that their knowledge of the incorporation was enough to make them blameworthy. They can hardly be chastised for finding the Salomon incorporation suspect. Indeed, their suspicions were confirmed by two different courts. But more striking is Lord Macnaghten's almost off-handed dismissal of the creditors' reliance on Aron's history of trustworthy dealing, as though years of trust built between trading partners do not form the basis for a reasonable expectation that debts will be repaid. On Macnaghten's account, it was Salomon and not the creditors who had 'been dealt with somewhat harshly'. And while he did voice his own view that the legal priority of debenture-holders over unsecured creditors was a 'scandal' that he did not have the power to change, his moral objections did not in any way attach to the erection of an entirely fictitious wall of insulation between existing trading partners.

This moral attitude of *caveat dantis* (i.e., lender beware) exemplifies the turning point that *Salomon* represents. Parliament did not expect their law to apply to the likes of Salomon,

FIGURE 5.3. Lord Macnaghten.

and neither did his creditors. Salomon's industry peers were shocked by his conduct. Lord Halsbury accused the lower courts of Monday-morning legislating, but the reality is that the House of Lords made a similar manoeuvre: they decided that the corporate veil was no longer a practical tool but a moral reality. Accordingly, the genealogy of the corporate veil reveals the inevitable circularity of Milton Friedman's now-hoary adage that if it is legal, then it is moral. In ascertaining when they might peer behind the veil, courts have been *creating* the law, not relying on it. If in business, all that is legal is moral, and in corporate law, all that is moral, for the purposes of the veil, is legal, then legality and morality are both up in the air. *Salomon*'s significance was in the Court's willingness to decide what, in effect, was moral business.

For all of its decisiveness, *Salomon* left a tangle of significant issues in its wake that have occupied the law's collective imagination and resolve. Every one of these, ultimately, is rooted in the same basic question of fairness that the courts and the litigants grappled with in 1896:

* *Can shareholders ever be liable for the company's antics?* – yes, in exceptional circumstances where there is an obvious fraud and the company is merely a sham or facade to cover or facilitate such wrongdoing;
* *When do the company's board of directors take personal responsibility for their decisions and actions on behalf of the company?* – Directors can occasionally be civilly and/or criminally liable for some decisions that they make outside their formal decision-making authority as directors;
* *What is the priority of claims between debenture-holders and unsecured creditors?* – In general, debenture-holders, like Aron Salomon, still have prior rights over ordinary trade creditors and shareholders;
* *Must a corporation have a certain level of capitalisation?* – This varies considerably from one jurisdiction to another. A few impose a minimum amount so as to cover foreseeable claims against the company, but many impose no requirement;
* *Can a corporation be found guilty of criminal conduct?* – The price of corporate personality is that criminal liability can be imposed upon companies. However, this still serves to protect the individuals (e.g., directors and managers) who are responsible for the offending company's decisions and actions; and
* *Do companies receive the benefits or protections of any constitutional rights?* – In many jurisdictions, corporations have secured for themselves the benefit of certain rights (e.g., search and seizure and freedom of expression).

As a contemporary example of the force of 'separate personality', the 1991 decision of the House of Lords in *Adams v.*

Cape Industries plc is typical. Adams worked for an American subsidiary of Cape Industries that was an English firm in the business of marketing asbestos. Adams became ill due to his exposure to asbestos dust. When he sought to sue the American corporation, he discovered that it had no assets to speak of. He therefore brought an action against Cape Industries directly and contended that the two companies should be treated as being part of one and the same economic enterprise. The courts decided that the action must fail as the two companies were entirely separate as a matter of law, even though it was accepted that the corporate structure between Cape Industries and its American subsidiary was designed to minimise legal liability and taxation. The road from *Salomon* is not difficult to trace, but it continues to be contentious in its direction and destination.

Accordingly, in important ways, it was the ethical dimension of *Salomon* that had the more lasting, if indirect effect. The effect of the House of Lords' decision was to give the act of incorporation its seal of moral approval. While the reliance on incorporation for overtly fraudulent purposes would still be treated as improper and unacceptable, the decision to incorporate would not necessarily be considered unethical even if it did, as in Aron Salomon's situation, bring hardship on the nascent company's creditors. *Salomon* helped to ensure that the nature of business was business, that business ethics only meant not acting fraudulently or illegally, and that traders and other businesspeople were responsible only for their own interests. If it ever existed, the idea that entrepreneurs should do more than pursue profit was laid to rest in *Salomon*. Since then, the whole debate around the corporate veil has pushed issues of ethical propriety to the margin. On some accounts, it has succeeded in ignoring them entirely.

CONCLUSION

Sadly, there was no happy ending for Aron: he suffered a stroke and was dead within a few months of the final decision in *Salomon*. He died *intestate* (without a will) on 13 May

1897 at age 60. As so often occurred, the children carried a heavy burden in continuing the family's commercial ventures; the name 'Salomon' was hardly a synonym for a solid investment opportunity. The family businesses in Northampton continued for a number of years but succumbed to much the same fate as the original venture. An 'A. Salomon & Co. Ltd.', having been formally dissolved in 1907, was resurrected by the Salomon brothers by 1912. They proceeded to see this and the rest of their ventures fail by 1915. The veil of incorporation may have parried some of the commercial blows that struck the family's footwear business, but it could not save it entirely from a continued economic onslaught. The idea of the 'company' still lives on, but this particular company soon received the proverbial boot.

But the *Salomon* litigation did not die with Aron. An action was brought for unpaid legal bills against Aron's estate by his lawyer, Ralph Raphael. *Re Raphael* was heard and decided in February 1899. His son Emanuel took up the litigation cudgels on his father's behalf and argued that, as a pauper, Aron should not be required to pay. Mr Justice Kekewich did not agree and ordered Raphael to be paid out of whatever was left in Aron's estate of £503. He reasoned that the upshot of *Salomon* was that 'though Aron was not thereby made a wealthy man, he was rehabilitated, and removed from the list of paupers'. So, Aron's triumph in *Salomon* was rendered somewhat Pyrrhic. He died much as he came to Whitechapel, with little wealth to his name. The fact that Aron's reputation lives on through legal history as the patron saint of all one-person companies would likely have been of little comfort to him and his family. Like so many others, he remains both victim and villain of this particular piece.

It would be heartening to conclude that the ghost of *Salomon* no longer inhabits the boardrooms and backrooms of companies. But that would be more wishful thinking than anything else – the notion that business ethics is more about business than ethics still holds true. While there is much talk about enhanced moral sensibilities in business dealings, there is little on actual display to support that; the shenanigans on

Wall Street and in the City of London in the early part of twenty-first century offer ample evidence of the unsettling reality behind the empty rhetoric. Although 'corporate social responsibility' is the new buzzword of the corporate market-place, it seems to be more about window-dressing than any substantive effort to transform business conduct and its controlling standards. Like 'Hell's Angels' and 'airline schedules', 'business ethics' is another candidate for the dictionary of oxymorons. This is to be regretted. And it would be reassuring to think that *Salomon*'s law lords might be less sanguine about the wisdom of their decision if they had known the kind of business ethics to which it has contributed.

6

FIFTY SHADES OF *Brown*

Consent and the criminal law

'Consent' is one of the most important yet most contested notions in all of law and society. So much is done and so much is justified in its name: bargains, elections, sporting contests, medical procedures, personal relations and the like. Even if people act against what is thought to be their own best and future interests, their consent or agreement is often treated as being sufficient to confer legitimate approval on the decision or course of action chosen. A bad decision and its consequences are not set aside or mitigated by that fact alone if a person is adjudged to have consented to it. Not surprisingly, with so much riding on it, there is heated debate over what can count as adequate and endorsing consent in specific situations. For instance, while it is thought that consent must be freely given and not induced by threat or deception, there is widespread disagreement over the precise terms for evaluating the presence and quality of such contextual and vitiating conditions. Furthermore, the conditions for identifying sufficient consent will vary in relation to exactly what action is being excused or allowed.

Of course, one of the most crucial areas in which consent plays a central role is the criminal law. If people are thought to have consented to certain interactions with others or interferences by them, then such activity is treated as beyond the reach or purview of criminal charges and sanctions. This is nowhere more significant than in the realm of sexual activity. However, apart from the difficult issues surrounding the question of what is to count as valid consent (e.g., must an alleged rapist simply have an honest belief as to consent being given or must it also be a reasonable belief as well?), the law has chosen to place important limits on what exactly can be consented to – if 'no' means 'no', what does 'yes' mean?

In a relatively recent decision, English law had to grapple with the onerous and divisive issue of whether adults could consent to serious harm and injury in the course of controversial sexual encounters. The resulting court decisions managed not only to highlight the analytical complexity of such questions, but also to capture the fraught political, social, moral and psychological terrain that courts have to map and traverse in deciding such matters. In a society that preaches tolerance and personal autonomy, the role of judges in determining what consenting adults can and cannot do in private is arguably as difficult as any they encounter.

A SPANNER IN THE WORKS

'It takes all sorts' is a tried-and-true Northern English expression. And that applies in spades to one of the great puzzles of human engagement – sex. People's preferences are varied and unfathomable from one to another. While physicality is all part and parcel of sexual relations, it can sometimes turn to more violent and dangerous pursuits: one person's pleasure can be another person's pain. In more extreme circumstances, this opens up to a world of sadomasochism in which the pain and pleasure become mixed together as process and performance in the pursuit of sexual gratification. And it was in the North of England that a group of men began to push the conventional envelope and challenge the limits of permissible and acceptable behaviour.

Since 1978, a number of gay men from all walks of life and all ages had been regularly convening in different houses to the northwest of industrial Manchester around the working-class suburbs of Bolton and Horwich. This locale is as far as away from the traditional fleshpots of cosmopolitan life as can be imagined. Nevertheless, over a period of ten years or so, they had engaged in varied and imaginative s/m exploits – bondage, waxing, whipping, lacerations, clamping, branding, nailing, sand-papering and the like – in a party atmosphere where fetish costumes were *de rigueur* and alcohol and drugs were liberally available. A few homes had been custom-fitted with dungeons and related paraphernalia. All the participants were willingly involved, sophisticated methods of passwords and code-words were used to ensure people had some ultimate control over what happened to them, and no one thought that they were acting in a criminal manner. Indeed, no one had to receive medical attention as a result of the sexual goings-on. Proceedings were videoed and the tapes were shared among the group, but no money exchanged hands.

In late 1987, Manchester Police raided some houses in another part of the city on an entirely unrelated matter. At one house, the officers came across a stash of videos that depicted identifiable men in a variety of graphic and violent activities. After close and extensive viewing, the Obscene Publications Squad came to the tentative conclusion that these videos were actually snuff films and that men were being tortured and mutilated before being killed; they did not imagine that anyone could or would consent to such activities. During the next year, more than 200 gay men were pulled in for questioning. In one case, so convinced were the police that murder had been committed, they dug up several gardens to look for buried bodies.

After an exhaustive murder investigation (costing upwards of £3 million) and titled Operation Spanner, the police decided that no homicides were committed. However, having discovered the location of the houses and the identity of many participants, they began to arrest and charge people in what was generally seen to be a face-saving exercise. In September 1989, sixteen men were charged with 'assaults causing actual bodily harm', 'aiding and abetting assaults', 'unlawful wounding', and 'keeping disorderly houses'. Another twenty-six were cautioned and released. The thrust of the charges was that they had 'kept a disorderly house to which numerous persons resorted in order to take part in acts of sadistic and masochistic violence and in accompanying acts of a lewd, immoral and unnatural kind'.

The salacious publicity accorded to these charges in the local and national press wreaked havoc on many of these men's lives. For instance, Roland Jaggard was a Group Head at British Aerospace where he worked on missile support systems. Once the 1987 raids become public and Roland's involvement was known, he began to be ostracised at work and received no merit pay. Not surprisingly, he went into a severe depression and his life began to fall apart. Upon being charged almost two years later in September 1989, the papers had a field day on him – one of the more sensational headlines was 'Top Scientist Arrested' and he was reported to have 'mutilated men's genitals'. The next day when he went into work, he was called into his boss's office and immediately dismissed. To add to his pain, his father died after a long illness and he had to take care of his distraught mother. Although he contemplated suicide, he clung to the idea that 'the most important thing in my life was my complete lack of guilt about any of the activities in which I had engaged'.

With an array of videos in evidence against them, the accused men conceded that the events had taken place. However, believing that they had done nothing wrong as everyone had knowingly consented to participate, they instructed counsel to argue that the charges against them should be stayed. The existing case-law on the role of consent in assault laws was dated and disjointed; much of it had occurred before any homosexual activity had been decriminalised. For instance, in the case of *Donovan* in 1934, a man was acquitted of indecent assault by caning on a young prostitute. The Court of Appeal held that where the act itself is unlawful, there is no need to prove a lack of consent; the existence of consent is a defence, not an element of the offence itself. However, lawful acts can become unlawful where there is no consent. The court came to the vague conclusion that 'lack of consent is *sometimes* an element of the offence which needs to be proved'. The *Brown* case offered an opportunity to give a little more clarity to the law.

Their trials took place in December 1990 at the Central Criminal Court or, as it is more commonly known, the Old Bailey. The judge assigned to the case was James Rant. A Cambridge graduate and seasoned barrister, he was appointed to the bench at the relatively young age of 48. He had a reputation for strict discipline and conservative views; he later became a senior military judge. He gave short shrift to the arguments that the consent of victims was a defence to criminal assault and related charges. Consequently, with little option, the defendants pleaded guilty in the hope that their mitigating pleas would lead to lighter punishments. They were to be seriously disappointed.

The leading and middle-aged organisers of the s/m activities were given harsh prison terms; they ranged from twelve months to four years and six months. Some were also ordered to reimburse legal aid to the tune of several thousand pounds. On passing sentence, Judge Rant commented that 'the unlawful conduct now before the court would be dealt with equally in the prosecution of heterosexuals or bisexuals if carried out by them: the homosexuality of the defendants is only the

FIGURE 6.1. The Old Bailey, London. Courtesy of Ben Sutherland / Flickr

background against which the case must be viewed'. The convicted men, many shaking and in tears, were taken down into the holding cells of the Old Bailey. A few hours later, they were taken to Wandsworth Prison to start their sentences. There, they were stripped, searched and given standard prisoner uniforms. However, they were considered vulnerable to attack by other prisoners; all were designated as Rule 43 prisoners and they were put in an isolated wing with child molesters, sex offenders and other so-called *nonces* 'for their own safety'. Locked in their cells for almost twenty-three hours a day (with no toilet facilities, except buckets), they were in a fearful and dreadful state.

Nevertheless, while some accepted their fate and pushed on through their sentences, five of them began an appeal – Anthony Brown, Colin Laskey, Saxon Lucas, Graham Cadman, and, of course, Roland Jaggard. They were determined to vindicate themselves and the legitimacy of the s/m practices in which they had willingly and enthusiastically participated. After lodging their appeal, they were granted bail and released after about six harrowing weeks in prison.

FIGURE 6.2. Wandsworth Prison, London. Courtesy of diamond geezer / Flickr

The appeal took place in early February 1992; it lasted three days and was presided over by the Chief Justice of England, Geoffrey Lane. He was a formidable figure who took a hard law-and-order stance throughout his career. He came in for considerable flack for his handling of two high-profile cases on the Irish bombers. Although he gave unconditional weight to police evidence, it was later revealed that police fabrication and tampering with evidence was rife in both cases. Also, in 1983, Lane had given a lecture at his *alma mater*, Cambridge University, in which he recommended that the word 'gay' should be abandoned and that 'homosexuals' or 'buggers' should be used instead. This was hardly an encouraging sign for Brown and his companions.

A couple weeks after the hearing on 19 February, the Chief Justice rendered the judgment of the court. He dismissed the appeals, but reduced significantly their sentences on the basis that they 'did not appreciate that their actions in inflicting injuries were criminal'. However, lest anyone would be tempted to take advantage of the courts' leniency in such matters, Chief Justice Lane added that 'in future, that argument will not be open to a defendant in circumstances such as these'.

The analytical push of Lane's opinion in affirming the guilt of Brown and his fellow criminals was that criminal sanctions attached to any assault likely to cause bodily harm (whether extreme or not) if it was not justified by 'good reason'. Yet, apart from offering examples such as sport and, more controversially, lawful chastisement, he was far from forthcoming about what amounts to a good reason. Indeed, he made the insubstantial and unconvincing riposte that it was not necessary to fix upon any general definition of 'good reason' because 'it is sufficient to say, so far as the instant case is concerned, that we agree with the learned trial judge that the satisfying of sado-masochistic libido does not come within the category of good reason nor can the injuries be described as merely transient or trifling'. Nevertheless, even though relying only on this hunch or instinctive sense of things, Lord Lane and his appellate confreres conceded and certified that a point of law of general public importance was involved and so an appeal to the House of Lords should go ahead.

A LORDLY AFFAIR

The publicity surrounding the fate of Brown and his s/m comrades was largely negative and disapproving. However, a loose affiliation of activists began to converge and offer vocal as well as funding support to the convicted men. The group took on the name Countdown on Spanner. Apart from galvanising backing for the quintet's forthcoming appeals, the collective sought to bring s/m activities out of the shadows and more into the mainstream. It campaigned with the ambition of demonstrating not only that such activities were more common among both straight and gay people than the police and courts assumed, but also that s/m offered a much safer alternative to intercourse in an age of HIV and AIDS. Bolstered by such support, Brown and his fellow s/m practitioners prepared for their appearance before the law lords with renewed, if short-lived optimism.

Back in temporary custody, Brown and his friends sat through four days of arguments in chambers at Westminster in early December 1992. Almost three months later, on 11 March 1993, with Brown and his colleagues back in custody again, the Judicial Committee of the House of Lords handed down its much awaited decision. By a slim majority of three to two, it was held that the s/m companions were guilty as charged. Ironically, the three older judges were in the majority and the two younger judges were in the minority. The majority held that, no matter how informed or willing, consent could not place certain assaults that occasioned actual bodily harm outside the scope of criminal liability and sanctions. Accordingly, the guilt and sentences of the convicted men were upheld.

All five of the law lords seemed to agree that many acts of violence were permissible if the recipient of the violence freely and fully consented, such as in surgery, tattooing or some contact sports. However, there was very little agreement on the limits to such consent and the rationale for such exceptions, especially involving sexual conduct. Each judge gave long and slightly different accounts of their reasons for deciding as they did.

- Lord Templeman was 73 and a former tax lawyer. In the earlier case of *Gillick*, he had decided that a 16-year-old girl needed her parents' consent before she could obtain contraceptives. In this case, he contended that consent for assaults causing bodily harm that are not in the public interest should be unlawful, although what was in 'the public interest' was to be determined on a case-by-case basis. Rejecting the argument that people should be able to do what they like with their own bodies and casting doubt on the validity of genuine consent in this case, he took a paternalistic approach and insisted that 'sado-masochism is not only concerned with sex, but also . . . with violence'. Finally, he made a distinction between 'incidental violence' and 'violence which is inflicted for the indulgence of cruelty'. For him, s/m practices amounted to a 'cult of violence' that had almost no sexual or social benefits.
- Lord Jauncey of Tullichettle was in his late sixties, a Scot, a former naval officer and held conservative views on family life and the role of women. He took a similar paternalistic line to Templeman and insisted that 'if the injury is of such a nature, or is inflicted under such circumstances, that its infliction is injurious to the public as well as to the person injured', it cannot be redeemed in the eyes of the criminal law. Maintaining that the fact there were no serious injuries sustained was more luck than judgment, he saw the s/m world as corrupting of society, especially young and impressionable men.
- Lord Lowry was also in his seventies, Northern Irish, about to retire and not given to liberal views. Taking the stance that 'sado-masochistic homosexual activity cannot be regarded as conducive to the enhancement or enjoyment of family life or conducive to the welfare of society', he was unprepared to add s/m practices to the list of those

otherwise criminal activities (e.g., surgery, boxing, prostitution, etc.) that could be saved by the participants' consent.

- Lord Mustill was in his early sixties and was not afraid to rock the legal boat, albeit in moderate fashion. In his dissenting opinion, he emphasised that the case was less about violence and more about 'the criminal law of private sexual relations, if about anything at all'. While he personally found the acts of Brown and his companions to be 'repugnant', he placed great weight on the need to respect people's private autonomy; the existing laws of violence did not apply to private consensual acts, especially if they only caused slight or transient harm.

- Lord Slynn of Hadley was the youngest judge at 63, lectured widely, and was something of a *bon vivant* by traditional judicial standards. Accepting that some line has to be drawn 'as to what can and as to what cannot be the subject of consent', he rejected the judicial paternalism of the majority. Instead, he proposed that the test should not be the financial cost to the health care system, but whether the acts were carried out in private or public; the fact that the activity involved men and women or only men was not an acceptable distinction. Consequently, he concluded that adults should be able to consent to assaults causing less than serious bodily harm.

While the others had already completed their sentences and so were free men, Anthony Brown and Roland Jaggard still had time to serve. They were shipped off to Brixton Prison to complete their sentences. Conditions were much better for them there than in Wandsworth; they shared a cell and were well treated by prison staff. After a couple of months, they were finally released. However, the experience meant that they never did engage in s/m activities again. As Roland Jaggard confessed, this was a cause of great anxiety for him: 'This s/m part of me is a fundamental part of my make-up as a human being. I think I am slowly falling apart with the internalized stress of the suppression. I shall be quite relieved when my time to die finally comes'.

A MEASURED BACKLASH

Predictably, the response to the decision of the law lords was wide and varied. A vocal and popular majority, fuelled by a sensationalist press, hailed the decision as a victory for common decency and traditional moral virtue. However, the chorus of more considered public and scholarly opinion was more questioning. Top of the list was the view that such sexual paternalism and prurience had little place in contemporary society; the values of the 1950s had little purchase or relevance to the 1990s. This was especially so when the paternalism was formulated and applied by a group of older white men who were not at all representative of society at large and whose values were sheltered behind the guise of 'legal reasoning'. If such s/m activities were to be criminalised, it demanded a more responsive and broad-based policymaking process. Moreover, the reasoning of the judges and their efforts at distinguishing s/m practices from more traditional dangerous pursuits, such as contact sports, was considered to be weak and unconvincing.

Apart from the dissenting judges' emphasis about respect for privacy in exercising sexual autonomy, many critics picked up on the sexual double standards being relied upon by the judges. At its bluntest, it was noted that the three judges in the majority seemed to be motivated by a barely disguised homophobia. Similar consensual activity by straight couples did not attract the same official or judicial sanction; non-consensual sex is as criminal as non-consensual s/m activity. For instance, in *Wilson* in 1996, the Court of Appeal overturned the conviction of a husband for branding his initials on his wife's buttocks on the basis that this was more a form of tattooing than sado-masochism and that 'consensual activity in the privacy of the matrimonial home was not a matter of criminal prosecution'.

Also, the characterisation of s/m practices as being as much about violence as sex was criticised as woefully unconvincing and in defiance of the participants' lived experience and expectations; it marginalises all forms of sexual activity that are not of a traditional heterosexual kind. Finally, the judgments in

Brown further emphasised that the line between so-called normal and deviant sexual practices is entirely contested and controversial; there is nothing given or settled about what does and does not count as normal sex other than what the majority of people do and think. This is the essence of a conformist and paternalistic approach to social behaviour.

Faced with such a barrage of legal and social critique, the Law Commission (a government group of legal experts charged with reforming law) almost immediately initiated a project aimed at re-evaluating the role of consent in assault laws. Eighteen months or so later, it announced in a consultation paper that s/m practices, if short of causing serious or permanently disabling injury, should be legal. However, while the government has not acted on such recommendations in changing the law, the criminal prosecution service and the lower courts have been much more reluctant to convict in similar circumstances to the activities of Brown and his colleagues. Although the majority judgment in *Brown* remains a formally ruling precedent, the views of the dissenting judges seem to have garnered more informal and practical support. For instance, in the 2013 case of *Lock*, a straight couple acted out an s/m scene from the novel *Fifty Shades of Grey*; the woman was chained and the man whipped her causing substantial bruising to her buttocks. In contrast to the logic of *Brown*'s majority, the man was acquitted.

Although the domestic criminal process had come to its ultimate conclusion with the House of Lords decision, a trio of the *Brown* defendants – Anthony Brown, Roland Jaggard and Colin Laskey – took their case to the European Court of Human Rights. They adopted the legal tack that the British government was in breach of Article 8 of the European Convention on Human Rights that guaranteed the privacy rights of individuals and that consensual sexual relations were within its ambit. After an elaborate appeal process and not unexpectedly, the Court unanimously ruled against Brown and Jaggard on 19 February 1997, ten years after the initial investigations began. Sadly, Laskey had died from a heart attack before the opinion could be rendered. The gist of the judgment was that a state had the power to regulate behaviour that might inflict physical or psychological harm and that there was no bias demonstrated against homosexuals in the enforcement of the existing laws. It was the legal end of a long road for Brown and his confreres.

Even today, the law on s/m practices remains murky. Exactly where the line is and should be drawn between those acts that can and cannot be consented to for matters of criminal prosecution is hard to pinpoint. The general consensus seems to be that consent can be a defence to assaults that lead to relatively minor and/or temporary injuries, but not for those that lead to serious or lasting injuries. So, in *Emmett* in 1999, a woman's consent to having lighter fluid poured over her breasts and lit did not operate as a defence for her partner as it resulted in serious injury and infection. However, in the 2004 case of *Dica*, it was decided that, although having sex knowing that you are HIV positive amounts to a serious assault, consent (i.e., agreeing to sex with knowledge that the other person is HIV positive) can be used as a defence.

Nevertheless, while the legal system had delivered its verdict, the struggle to receive wider acknowledgement for s/m practices continued in the important tribunals of public opinion. Although Anthony Brown and Roland Jaggard were exhausted by their ordeals, they became figureheads and heroes for the s/m movement; they received various awards from gay and s/m lobby groups. There were demonstrations and marches in London; s/m clubs became more common and less secretive. The Spanner Trust remains a leading campaigner for the rights of adults to engage in consensual s/m activities. Although the criminal battle had been lost, the war for sexual freedom was slowly and not always surely being advanced. The party boys from Bolton and Manchester had left their own indelible mark on the social and erotic scene.

At the initial trial at the Old Bailey, Roland Jaggard had made the ironic aside that, while their own preference for fetish clothing (e.g., leather, rubber, etc.) had been viewed as a mark of their deviance, the judges and barristers themselves were partial to their own fetish uniforms of wigs, robes, fancy

FIGURE 6.3. Roland Jaggard, Ian Gurnhill of the Spanner Trust and Tony Brown. Courtesy of the Spanner Trust

shoes, etc. Jaggard's comments underlined the fact that, as with so much else, context and setting are everything when it comes to physical and sexual relations. Attributing blame and inflicting punishment are the privilege of some and the burden of others. For all the pain that they unwittingly endured at the hands of the legal process, Anthony Brown and his s/m friends still have no definitive answer to what they can and cannot do in their private lives. Whatever one thinks of their s/m preferences, they surely deserve a better fate than that.

CONCLUSION

As will be obvious, the judges have struggled to negotiate a sensible and acceptable path through the maze of consent, sex, and the criminal law. While it is clear most of the time that 'no' means 'no', it still remains unclear what 'yes' means. If *Brown* and its legal progeny have anything to tell us, it is that 'yes' is only another way of saying 'maybe' in the eyes of the criminal law: there is no certain or compelling answer to what persons can and cannot consent to in their private pursuit of sexual fulfilment. It would seem that the more a person's route to sexual gratification diverges from what others are doing, the more is the chance that they will be straying into the half-light of penal prohibition where what is permissible and impermissible is shifting and unstable. Accordingly, in terms of the criminal law, the best that can be said is that what amounts to 'safe sex' remains a puzzle that is unlikely to be solved for decades to come.

7

PUTTING UP A DEFENCE

Sex, murder and videotapes

The legal profession is not the most beloved of vocations. From Plato through William Shakespeare and Charles Dickens to Tom Wolfe and John Grisham, literature attests to its impugned status. Matters are not much different in real life. In the public's mind, lawyers are perceived as being not only adept at the dubious arts of manipulation and double dealing but also moral hypocrites because they defend these practices in the brazen name of 'professional ethics'. Along with used car dealers and telemarketers, lawyers are considered to be among the least trustworthy and least respected of all professionals. Lord Bolingbroke's assessment of the legal profession several centuries ago remains true today: 'the profession of law, in its nature the noblest and most beneficial to mankind, is in its abuse an abasement of the most sordid and pernicious kind'.

If the legal profession at large suffers from bad press, the criminal bar is the butt of the most insistent criticism. The ethical history of criminal lawyering is populated by a cast of colourful characters – from the ennobled image of Clarence Darrow to the more dubious persona of Johnnie Cochrane. People tend to identify defence lawyers with their unsavoury clients and their unforgivable deeds. However, when individuals are in trouble, they want the best and most dogged lawyers on their side and their side alone; they need to be assured about the unquestioned loyalty of their lawyer to their cause. Whatever the rap against the legal profession generally, accused persons want their lawyer to do all that they can to raise every issue and argument in an uncompromising way that affords them every chance of acquittal.

This push and pull puts criminal defence lawyers in an ethical and professional bind. They must juggle competing obligations to their clients, the courts, the legal profession and the public interest. And this is no mean feat. Often misunderstood in actions and motivations, criminal lawyers are there to defend their clients, not to judge them. Indeed, the mantra of the defence bar is that they 'lend their exertions to all, and themselves to none'. Because accused persons are presumed innocent and entitled to a fair trial, the lawyer is required to challenge the Crown's case in the most vigorous and partial way. Against such a backdrop, criminal defence lawyers have to tread a very thin line between zealous advocacy and unethical conduct. Of course, it is not at all surprising that some have overstepped that line.

Two decades ago, there was a notorious Canadian case that put the ethical practice of criminal lawyers under official and public scrutiny. So difficult and sordid were its circumstances that it divided the profession about what lawyers can and should do in mounting a defence for their clients. In a case about sex, murder and videotapes, a lawyer was placed in the invidious position of having to decide how he should handle his competing duties to the private interests of his client and the public interests of justice. How far can lawyers go in defending their clients without obstructing the pursuit of justice? The fact that lawyers still disagree about what lawyers should do in such circumstances only adds to the significance and status of the case in the legal canon.

A SORDID TALE

In February 1993, Kenneth Murray received a collect call from Paul Bernardo who sought his legal assistance. Bernardo had been given Murray's name by a family member and a friend.

Murray was a sole practitioner in Newmarket, a small Ontario town close to Toronto. He had been in practice for about ten years and was certified as a specialist in criminal litigation. Although he had extensive experience in criminal courts, he mostly did run-of-the-mill legal aid work. In accepting to act for Bernardo, Murray became involved in a series of events that was to make grisly headlines in the popular and professional press for several years to come. While Bernardo was ultimately convicted of both rape and murder, Murray was himself charged with 'obstructing justice'.

When Bernardo made that initial call to Murray, he was in serious trouble. He had been arrested for a series of rapes in Scarborough, a Toronto suburb. As if this was not troubling enough, Bernardo was also under suspicion for at least a couple of murders that had occurred earlier in St Catherines, a small town about fifty kilometres from Toronto, where he and his wife, Karla Homolka, lived. The circumstances of those criminal charges provide a nauseating and dreadful backdrop against which Murray's professional integrity and judgment would be called into severe question. Regretfully, Murray assumed an important and detrimental role in how this sordid drama played out.

Bernardo was no ordinary criminal. Not only did he participate in some particularly gruesome rapes and murders, but he also did not fit what many considered to be the image of a sadistic killer. With boyish charm and good looks, he was a trainee accountant who presented as a likeable boy next door. However, behind that face was a tormented young man who was brought up in a highly dysfunctional family and who had been abused by his stepfather. While he had a reputation as something of 'a ladies man', his relations with woman were far from pleasant or straightforward. Once he hooked up with a certain Karla Homolka, Bernardo found a perverse kindred spirit with whom he could fulfil his darkest fantasies.

In October 1987, 23-year-old Bernardo met a 17-year-old Homolka in a hotel coffee shop, and they instantly bonded. Whether Homolka knew or not, Bernardo had already raped several women. They were soon engaged and set to marry;

they presented as an enviable Ken and Barbie couple. However, Bernardo was troubled that Homolka was not a virgin when they first met. So, on Christmas Eve 1990, by way of recompense, Homolka offered up her virgin 15-year-old sister, Tammy, as a peace offering and early Christmas present. Homolka drugged her sister and Bernardo raped her while she was unconscious. As cruel fate would have it, Tammy choked on her own vomit while she was unconscious and died. After an elaborate cover-up, the death was ultimately ruled accidental. However, as part of their nefarious scheme, they videotaped the whole affair. It was this act of vicious and voyeuristic vanity that would prove to be their end and, as circumstances would have it, Ken Murray's undoing.

A fortnight before their wedding in June 1991, Bernardo and Homolka escalated their sadistic activities by abducting a young 14-year-old girl, Leslie Mahaffy. She was tortured, raped and killed. The degradation was made into a video recording. Later that month, her concrete-encased body was found dumped in a nearby lake. About nine months later in April 1992, the couple kidnapped 15-year-old Kristen French at gunpoint in a local church parking lot. This time, she was held for three days, during which she was also tortured, raped and then killed. Again, the confinement was videotaped by Bernardo and Homolka. French's body was found two weeks later in a ditch. One other woman was abducted, but she managed to escape.

By this time, the police were closing in on Bernardo. But the case against him was far from made out. However, after a three-year investigation, the police had enough evidence to arrest Bernardo for the Scarborough rapes. While he was in custody, Bernardo retained Ken Murray as his lawyer. At the same time, the police obtained a warrant to search the home of Bernardo and Homolka who were the prime suspects in the murders of Mahaffy and French. It was at this stage that Murray found himself faced with a dilemma that would haunt him and the legal profession to this day.

In May 1993, after a ten-week search of the house from which no tapes were located, the police contacted Murray to

FIGURE 7.1. House shared by Paul Bernardo and Karla
Homolka at 57 Bayview Drive, Port Dalhousie, Ontario.
Courtesy of Toronto Star

ask if his client wanted any personal belongings from the
house. On 6 May, Murray went to the house with Carolyn
MacDonald (a young lawyer with whom Murray shared office
space and, on occasion, files, now including the Bernardo one)
and Kim Doyle (his office manager and law clerk). He had
received written instructions from Bernardo to retrieve the
videotapes that had been hidden in the bathroom ceiling
behind a light fixture. While it is unclear whether Murray
and Bernardo spoke by cell phone while Murray was in the
house, what is clear is that Murray located the six 8-mm
videotapes. Excited that he had unearthed 'a bonanza' and 'a
gold mine', he followed Bernardo's instructions and made the
fateful decision to take the tapes with him. However, while he
made copies of the tapes, he did not view them immediately.
Instead, he stashed them in his office safe where he kept them
for the next seventeen months.

By this time, the police were convinced that Bernardo and
Homolka were responsible for Mahaffy and French's
murders. However, lacking any definitive evidence against
them, the police felt that they had little choice other than to

make a plea bargain with Homolka who had become disaffected with Bernardo after he had seriously assaulted her. So, on 14 May, a week after Murray had located the tapes, a written agreement was signed whereby, in return for giving extensive and damning evidence against Bernardo, Homolka would plead guilty to the lesser charges of manslaughter for the deaths of French and Mahaffy; the Crown would only seek a sentence of twelve years' imprisonment. Importantly, it was clear that no deal would have been made if the tapes had been available to the police or prosecutors. This bargain became known as 'The Deal with The Devil'.

Although Murray did not know that such a plea bargain was in the immediate works, he realised that such a deal had been made when, in the following week on 18 May, Bernardo was charged with two counts of first-degree murder. As a result, Murray's retainer was extended by Bernardo to cover these charges. At this pivotal moment, Murray was instructed by Bernardo to view the tapes and to utilise them as best he could to defend him. Two of the six tapes offered graphic evidence of the rape and torture of Mahaffy and French by Bernardo and Homolka. However, there was no direct depiction on the tapes of the killings themselves or who did them.

So educated and with Bernardo's supporting instructions, Murray determined that it might be possible to utilise what was on the tapes to defend Bernardo. His apparent plan was to contend that, while Bernardo was guilty of the rapes, he was not the exclusive or leading perpetrator of the murders – that was the prime responsibility of the duplicitous Homolka who was less the abused spouse and more the leading malefactor. This seemed an odd strategy because, amongst other things, Murray did nothing to intervene in Homolka's hearing in July 1993 when she pled guilty to two counts of manslaughter and received a twelve year jail term. If Murray had revealed his custody of the tapes, the deal might not have gone through and Homolka would be less able to downplay her role in the deaths of Mahaffy and French.

Nevertheless, Murray held on to the tapes through the remainder of 1993 and into 1994. During this time, Bernardo flip-flopped on what his defence should be and how the tapes should be handled. However, when Bernardo instructed Murray that he would deny any involvement in the abduction, let alone the murder of Mahaffy and French, and that the tapes should remain concealed indefinitely from the police or anyone else, Murray decided that he should no longer continue as Bernardo's lawyer. He took the view that he could no longer provide a full and vigorous defence as professional integrity demanded that, once he knew beyond a doubt that Bernardo was involved in the rapes and murders, he should withdraw. Murray's decision was reinforced in July when he received test results from a sample of vomit that showed a DNA match between Bernardo and French.

Accordingly, in August 1994, Murray asked John Rosen, a very experienced criminal defence lawyer, to take on the case. Although Rosen agreed to take on the case, Murray did not initially inform him that he still had the 'lost tapes' in his possession. What he did do was retain another lawyer, Austin Copper, as his own counsel, and sought his confidential advice on what to do about the tapes. After consultations with the Law Society of Upper Canada (Ontario's governing body), it was decided that the tapes should be handed over to Rosen as Bernardo's new counsel. After viewing them and making unsuccessful efforts to cut any kind of plea bargain for Bernardo, Rosen delivered the tapes to the police on 22 September 1994.

In summer of 1995, Bernardo was tried and convicted for the murders of Mahaffy and French. On 1 September 1995, he was sentenced to life without parole for twenty-five years. The tapes were used at trial and Homolka gave strong evidence against Bernardo as the guilty party in both orchestrating the entire wretched saga and murdering the victims. Despite concerted efforts to nullify Homolka's plea bargain and relatively light sentence, the deal remained in place. However, although he had not been part of the action for many months, Ken Murray was far from done with the whole Bernardo/Homolka affair.

FIGURE 7.2. John Rosen. Courtesy of Rosen Naster LLP

OBSTRUCTING JUSTICE?

In the criminal process, the basic thrust of professional ethics is that, while prosecutors have a duty to ensure that the truth is exposed in court, defence counsel have no such duty. The responsibility of criminal defence lawyers is specific and specialised – they must take all possible steps to raise a reasonable doubt about the client's guilt; it is not to prove the accused person's innocence. Many rights are given to the accused and it is for defence lawyers to ensure those rights are respected. While there might be a general public concern with whether the accused 'did it', the focus of defence lawyers is more limited and must be focused on the legal guilt of their accused clients. In an adversarial system, each accused person is entitled to have his or her own champion whose loyalty is to the cause of the accused and to no one else. Criminal defence lawyers are in the business of advocacy, not judgment. Nevertheless, the fact that an accused person is entitled to as strong a defence as possible does not thereby translate into an invitation to counsel to do anything and everything to avoid conviction. The critical challenge is to establish what the ethical limits are on the methods and strategies that can be used to achieve that goal.

In being the 'zealous advocate' of their client, criminal lawyers must do all they can to seek an acquittal for their clients by 'fair and honourable means' and 'without illegality': nothing that lawyers as lawyers do becomes lawful by that fact alone. But, in doing so, they must also treat the court with 'candour, fairness, courtesy and respect'. This general injunction pulls in a number of different directions and places a considerable burden on defence counsel to juggle the competing obligations to clients, courts and society generally. That said, the dominant duty, to which the others function as limits, is well expressed by an English judge who said that advocates are expected 'fearlessly to raise every issue, advance every argument, and ask every question . . . which will help [their clients'] case and to obtain for clients the benefit of any and every remedy and defence which is authorized by law'.

A major source of difficulty for criminal lawyers flows from their general duty of confidentiality to clients. Except where future serious harm to another is about to be done, lawyers must not divulge any communications between themselves and their clients. When this is combined with the fact that defence lawyers are generally under no obligation to assist the prosecution in making its case by making available incriminating evidence otherwise unknown to the prosecution, the difficulties are further increased. A prominent commentator has suggested that it creates 'the lawyer's trilemma' – the lawyer has a duty to know everything, to keep it in strict confidence and to reveal it to the court. Nevertheless, although some disagree, the traditional wisdom is that, while lawyers are free and often obliged to challenge all the prosecution's evidence (even if they think that it is likely true), they cannot put forward affirmative defences (alibis, duress, etc.) if they have no reasonable basis in fact or allow their clients to offer perjured evidence. Even if lawyers withdraw from the case, they must maintain their clients' confidences.

This competition between competing duties of zealous advocacy, client confidentiality and court candour is particularly acute in regard to physical evidence (murder weapon, clothing, etc.). Because confidentiality attaches only to communications between lawyers and clients, it does not extend to the physical evidence of a crime itself. If lawyers come into possession of articles that they know are incriminating and will be beneficial to the prosecution, they cannot destroy or conceal them. Such evidence must be handed over to the police or the appropriate authorities. However, lawyers are obliged to take all efforts to keep confidential the source of the evidence that is turned over to the police or other authority. To preserve confidentiality as best as possible in such circumstances, the most desirable course is to turn over the physical evidence to an intermediary (e.g., another lawyer or the law society), which can then pass the evidence to the police without revealing who or where it came from. Nevertheless, this duty to disclose confidential information has been traditionally interpreted to be very limited in scope and is considered to apply only to physical evidence that can reasonably be considered to be the instrumentalities of crime (e.g., weapons or equipment) or the proceeds of crime (e.g., stolen money or property). While criminal lawyers must advise clients not to destroy or conceal evidence themselves, lawyers cannot disclose such communications to anyone about the fact of destruction or the location of concealment.

All these matters came into play in Ken Murray's defence of Bernardo. The main fact, of course, was that Murray had hidden the whereabouts of the incriminating tapes for seventeen months. However, there were several factors that took this case out of the ordinary: Murray was following his client's confidential instructions; the tapes were not an instrumentality of the crime; he came across them after being invited to his client's house by the police and after an extensive search by them; the tapes were possibly seen as being both inculpatory and exculpatory in content; and he always intended to hand over the tapes. Taken together, these facts muddy what is already a very murky set of ethical and professional waters.

In January 1997, eighteen months after Bernardo had been convicted, charges were brought against both Ken Murray and his co-counsel, Carolyn MacDonald. The gist of the indictment was that, by virtue of viewing the tapes and keeping their whereabouts secret, they had committed the crimes of obstructing justice and possessing child pornography. As well, Murray became the subject of complaints to the Law Society of Upper Canada. As a result, it decided to pursue charges of professional misconduct against Murray. While all criminal charges against Murray's co-counsel were later dropped as well as most of the criminal charges against Murray, the authorities refused to set aside Murray's obstruction of justice charges.

It was not until June 2000 that Ken Murray went on trial and offered the courts the opportunity to clear up matters. Pleading 'not guilty', Murray realised that he was in for the fight of his professional life and reputation. The proceedings took place before Justice Patrick Gravely in the Ontario Superior Court of Justice in Toronto; he was a seasoned judge and amateur vintner who was coming to the end of a long and pioneering judicial career. Murray was charged under s.139(2) of Canada's Criminal Code. It stated that 'everyone who willfully attempts . . . to obstruct, pervert or defeat the course of justice is guilty of an indictable offence and liable to imprisonment for a term not exceeding ten years'. After hearing arguments and careful consideration, Justice Gravely was insistent that he was only concerned with the criminal status of Murray's action: 'I want to make clear that my function in this case is limited to deciding if Murray has committed the crime of attempting to obstruct justice, not to judge his ethics'.

The judge took the view that Murray's concealment of the tapes for seventeen months constituted an improper and continuing interference with the operation of the justice system. However, he was not convinced that the Crown had demonstrated beyond a reasonable doubt that Murray had the specific intent to do so 'wilfully' as was required to turn this

FIGURE 7.3. Ken Murray. Courtesy of Toronto Star

misguided action into a criminal offence. In legal parlance, he committed the offence's *actus reus* (i.e., guilty act), but did not exhibit the necessary *mens rea* (i.e., guilty mind). Accordingly, Murray was acquitted. In reaching this decision, Justice Gravely made several important findings that not only explicated the crime of obstructing justice, but also touched upon the ethical obligations of legal counsel. Indeed, he was of the firm opinion that, while Murray had not acted in line with the ethical expectations of the legal profession, he was sufficiently, if wrongly confused about his ethical and legal obligations that he should not be subject to criminal sanctions.

For Justice Gravely, it was crucial that a distinction be drawn between conversations about the tapes and the handling of the tapes. All communications between Bernardo and Murray fell under the umbrella of solicitor–client privilege and could not be divulged by Murray; this included any discussion about the tapes and the use to which they were to be put. Nonetheless, the location and concealment of the tapes raised a very different set of issues. While defence counsel are under no obligation to assist the police in their investigations, he opined that they cannot and must not take steps to keep so-called real or physical evidence out of the police's hands. However, the professional rules are far from clear in their intent and scope. Moreover, the judge accepted that Murray did intend to reveal the tapes and their contents at trial in order to cross-examine Homolka and/or to raise a reasonable doubt about whether Bernardo had actually killed the victims. As Justice Gravely concluded:

> While Murray made only a token effort to find out what his obligations were, had he done careful research he might have remained confused. The weight of legal opinion . . . is to the effect that lawyers may not conceal material physical evidence of crime, but how this rule applies to particular facts has been the subject of extensive discussion.

The response to Justice Gravely's decision and judgment was decidedly lukewarm. A common observation was that he had given lawyers too much leeway by allowing Murray to rely on ignorance of the law; this defence is not available to most accused persons, only a mistake of fact can be relied upon as a valid excuse for what would otherwise be criminal conduct. This error was compounded by the fact that Murray had made no genuine effort to research the legal and professional expectations in regard to the concealment of the tapes. Also, the fact that the Crown did not appeal the decision on a point of law suggests to some that the legal community was accepting of a decision that seemed to extend special protections to lawyers from obstruction of justice charges. Therefore, the decision did little to assuage public opinion about the performance of lawyers in the whole Bernardo-Homolka saga.

ETHICAL IMPASSE

As if the challenges facing criminal defence lawyers were not difficult enough, the confusion surrounding the circumstances about when and how they should hand over incriminating evidence to the police or prosecution makes their task doubly hard. It must be remembered that ensuring that lawyers act properly is not only a matter of professional propriety, but also can directly and decisively affect the fate of persons accused with crimes. The dilemma is that if lawyers fail to disclose to the investigating authorities inculpatory material evidence against their clients, they risk professional and criminal sanction; if lawyers do hand over such incriminating evidence, they might also sell their clients down river and also face professional discipline for so doing. Although being able to draw the line between the two seems a necessary and desirable condition for criminal defence work, that task calls into play foundational understandings of lawyers' ethical duties. Yet its satisfactory fulfilment has eluded many law societies and professional organisations.

Accordingly, while the trial determined Murray's criminal responsibility, little was clarified about the professional and ethical quality of his actions. Despite the implicit plea by Justice Gravely for greater clarity about the relevant professional rules of ethical conduct, the Law Society decided six months later to withdraw any charges of professional misconduct. This left something of an ethical black hole into which lawyers could fall. Although all lawyers agree that lawyers must not take active steps to conceal physical evidence from the investigating authorities, there remains a wide division of professional opinion about the precise operation and parameters of this directive. In short, Gravely had set the ethical stage but he had not scripted the dramatic action: both lawyers and, as importantly, accused persons remained in the dark about their rights and responsibilities.

Of course, other jurisdictions have grappled with this professional quandary of legal ethics. While most adopt a similar core of solutions and values, there is an important division of opinion over some of the more tricky issues. The leading American authority is the Washington case of *Olwell* in 1964. A lawyer was given a gun by his client; it was likely the weapon used by his client in a murder. The lawyer claimed that he was under no obligation to hand over the gun to the police. The court decided that the lawyer–client privilege did not apply and that the lawyer should not hold on to the weapon:

The attorney should not be a depository for criminal evidence (such as a knife, other weapons, stolen property, etc.), which in itself has little, if any, material value for the purposes of aiding counsel in the preparation of the defence of his client's case. Such evidence given the attorney during legal consultation for information purposes and used by the attorney in preparing the defence of his client's case, whether or not the case ever goes to trial, could clearly be withheld for a reasonable period, should, as an officer of the court, on his own motion turn the same over to the prosecution.

However, in the later Californian case of *Meredith* that drew some close parallels with Murray's dilemma, a client told his lawyer that the victim's wallet in a murder case had been thrown away behind the client's home. The lawyer hired someone to recover the wallet and bring it to his office. After examining the wallet, the lawyer handed it over to police. At trial, the police sought to call the person who had retrieved the wallet and have him testify to the location of the wallet. The lawyer contended that, while the prosecution could enter the wallet in evidence, it could not reveal the location where the wallet was found as the source of that information was a privileged communication from the accused client. The court rejected that claim as the lawyer had interfered with the wallet and prevented the police from locating it themselves: the wallet and its location were used to obtain a conviction.

All this suggests several things about what Murray should have done. First, it is clear that he should have realised at an early stage that he was out of his depth; he had little experience of dealing with high-profile and complicated murder cases. His ethical duty was to withdraw from the case so that Bernardo could obtain a more competent counsel. The fact he came to this realisation eighteen months into the case when he decided to pull out and hand Bernardo's defence over to John Rosen merely confirms his failing; Murray did a disservice to his client, himself and the legal profession generally.

Secondly, a rudimentary sense of the professional rules and prevailing wisdom would have warned Murray about the danger of going to Bernardo's house and checking out the whereabouts of the tapes. Simply because he received instructions for Bernardo to do so does not validate or justify such actions. The most appropriate and ethical course to follow would have been for Murray to inform Bernardo that, if he retrieved the tapes, he would most likely be under an obligation to hand them over to the police. Consequently, he should have advised his client that, all things considered, the most beneficial action would be to let sleeping dogs lie. After all, Murray was obliged not to reveal any communications with Bernardo about the whereabouts of the tapes and the police had indicated that they would demolish the house after Murray's visit (as they did). In this way, the tapes would never be found and Murray would not be implicated in their concealment or destruction. While this course of action might not have endeared Murray to the public, it would have been the least worst way of satisfying the competing demands placed upon him.

Thirdly, even if Murray had taken the fraught step of removing the tapes from Bernardo's house, he could have still managed to act within the bounds of professional integrity. He could have held them for a short amount of time, viewed them and then handed them over to the police or Crown; it was holding on to them for eighteen months that was Murray's downfall, not his retrieval of them. In this way, he would have been able to satisfy himself that there was or was not something exculpatory about the tapes' contents and prepare a defence of Bernardo accordingly. If Bernardo had persisted in his instructions that Murray should not view them, Murray would have been obliged to hand them over immediately without viewing. However, the one fly in the ointment is that, in the days following Murray's retrieval of the tapes, Homolka had made her plea bargain with the police. Even assuming that Murray's claim that he did not hear of that fact until later was true, he could have ensured that he handed the tapes over in short order and certainly before Homolka's sentencing a couple of months later.

However, what does remain contested is whether Murray was entitled to visit the house, locate the tapes and verify to Bernardo that they were still there, and leave them exactly where they were. While it is clear that Murray had to keep confidential any communications with Bernardo about the tapes, it is unclear whether his actions of visiting the house and actually seeing the tapes, even touching them, puts him in a different position – was there any obligation on Murray to report the tapes' location to the police?

A similar situation arose in New York in the case of *Belge* in 1975 (a.k.a., The Buried Bodies Case). A lawyer was told by his client about the location of certain bodies that he had murdered and buried. The lawyer visited the site, saw the bodies and took photographs; he did not reveal this information or photographs to anyone. At his client's trial, he utilised this knowledge to support his defence that the client was insane. Following a public outcry, he was charged with failing to provide a decent burial for a dead person. The lawyer's defence was that, because he had not disturbed or relocated the bodies and made it more difficult for the police to locate them, he had acted entirely professional; he was under an ethical obligation both not to reveal this privileged information and not to do something that would incriminate his own client. The trial court accepted this argument and held that the lawyer had 'conducted himself as an officer of the court with all the zeal at his command to protect the constitutional rights of his client . . . and the interests of justice'.

In Ken Murray's situation, therefore, a strong argument can be made that he was not in breach of his professional duties if he had located the tapes and left them where they were. In so doing, he would not be obstructing justice, but simply failing to come forward with information. Whether he (or any one, including non-lawyers) are expected to volunteer such information is a moot point. Some lawyers insist that, once they move outside the realm of privileged communications, lawyers might actually have a higher responsibility in such circumstances than ordinary citizens. But this is far from a settled or majority position. What is sure is that, if he had acted in this way, Murray would still have been the target of public condemnation for his failure to act in what was considered the right thing to do. Yet this speaks as much to the gap between lawyers' and citizens' understanding of the expectations of lawyers' professional and ethical commitments.

The *Murray* case highlights the fact that the challenges to the criminal bar in meeting its ethical and professional responsibilities are difficult and many. It is relatively easy for counsel, as Murray did, to drift into a professional stance that shirks questions of ethical significance and simply muddles through. However, criminal lawyers can and should do a vigorous and committed job for their accused clients without fear that they are acting unethically. If there is one area of law where lawyers must court considerable ethical risks in the name of greater professional and social values, it is in the criminal process. While it might not be acceptable to think that it is right that 'a man should, with a wig on his head, and a band round his neck, do for a guinea what, without those appendages, he would think it wicked and infamous to do for an empire', it might perhaps be that 'not merely believing but knowing a statement to be true, he should do all that can be done by sophistry, by rhetoric, by solemn asseveration, by indignant exclamation, by gesture, by play of features, by terrifying one honest witness, by perplexing another, to cause a jury to think that statement false'. Thomas Macaulay saw the ethical opaqueness in all this. Perhaps we should too.

CONCLUSION

As might be expected, there are no happy endings to a sordid saga like this. The infamous tapes were destroyed in December 2001, although there are still lingering suggestions that a copy remains at large. Ken Murray quickly returned to the relative obscurity of small-town criminal law practice; his brush with celebrity status was chastening to say the least. Paul Bernardo remains locked up in a small segregated cell from which he is released for an hour's exercise each day. Initially housed in the old Kingston Penitentiary, he is now at the high-security

Millhaven Institution in Bath, Ontario, and is eligible for a faint-hope parole hearing in 2020. As for Karla Homolka, she was released from prison on 4 July 2005. She has since remarried, had three children with the brother of her Quebec lawyer, Thierry Bordelais, moved to the Caribbean and changed her name to Leanne.

The Bernardo-Homolka case stands out as one of, if not the most, gruesome episode in Canada's criminal annals. Its facts have been utilised as storylines in various TV dramas, including *Law & Order, Close to Home* and *Inspector Linley Mysteries*. There was also a movie made, titled *Karla*, that received limited release in Canada in the mid-2000s. Ontario's then premier, Dalton McGuinty, encouraged a boycott of the movie and it fared poorly. Nonetheless, a year does not pass in which mention is made of the case and its traumatising effect on the Canadian public imagination. However, despite all this and many promises to the contrary, the Law Society of Upper Canada (and the national Federation of Law Societies) never did live up to its promise to amend its rule and clarify the responsibilities of criminal defence lawyers in regard to physical evidence – when and how should they deal with physical evidence that comes to their attention or possession? This omission is a cheerless and unnecessary footnote to a thoroughly nauseating story of sex, lies and videotapes.

8

Wade-ING INTO CONTROVERSY

A case of accidental activism

The Supreme Court of the United States is no stranger to controversy. Its history is full of cases that have plunged the court into moral and social dilemmas of the most heated kind. As such, the justices have waded into or been thrust into deciding matters where others have feared (or been wise not) to tread. Unsurprisingly, some of its decisions have served to fan the flames of discord rather than douse them. Yet the US Supreme Court, like other highest courts of common law countries, has retained popular respect because it has managed to take a Goldilocks-style approach – not too far ahead of public opinion and not too far behind. While it might not always have been 'just right' in its decisions and opinions, it has succeeded in spotting and riding the incoming tide of social change in contentious matters, like school desegregation and gay rights.

However, one area of controversy that refuses to resolve itself or go away is abortion. It remains one of the most hotly contested areas on the social, moral, political and constitutional agenda. Despite the Supreme Court's 1973 decision to establish and protect a right for women to obtain an abortion, the debate around the existence and extent of such a right remains more embittered then ever. Indeed, the Supreme Court's decision in *Roe v. Wade* (and its legal repercussions) has become something of a lightning rod for supporters and opponents of a woman's right to choose. Whereas some harangue the decision for providing any constitutional protection for women's right to terminate a pregnancy, others criticise it for its failure to provide a compelling and solid basis for securing that right. All in all, the *Roe* decision has succeeded in satisfying few and alienating many.

In spite of or perhaps because of its notoriety, *Roe v. Wade* is accepted as one of the common law's greatest cases. It demonstrates a whole host of insights about the dynamics of the common law, especially in the constitutional cauldron of common law decision making – that, while law rules society, law itself is a product of that society and it will only be as effective in ruling society as society allows; that the most obscure litigants can become accidental activists in the development of the law; that judges can often be unlikely revolutionaries in pushing the law forward; and that nothing is final in the world of constitutional law. The background, decision and aftermath of *Roe* are the stuff of common law legend.

MEXICO AND EVERYTHING AFTER

Sarah Ragle was a 21-year-old Texan and one of only forty women in her law school cohort of 1,600 when she entered the University of Texas in 1965. She came from a middle-class family; her father was a Methodist pastor and her mother a local teacher. While a law student, she discovered in her third year of law school that she was pregnant. Realising that she was not ready to marry and that, as an unwed mother, she would have to drop out of law school, she decided to seek an abortion. Abortion was illegal in Texas at that time except if the mother's life was at risk. So she crossed the border into Mexico and had an abortion in a private clinic in Piedras Negras at a cost of $400. Fortunately, all went well and she returned to university to complete her law studies in good health and no longer pregnant.

Although she later married her boyfriend, Ron Weddington, this experience left a mark on Sarah. Not all women could afford to travel outside Texas and pay for an abortion. On her return to law school and after graduation, she began working with an underground abortion referral network that helped local women to access illegal but safe abortion clinics. She joined forces with Linda Coffee, another young lawyer, who had clerked for a rare female Federal judge and was practicing law in Dallas. Learning that constitutional challenges were underway in other states, they decided that they should bring a constitutional action against the repressive Texan laws. This meant that they needed to find a willing and suitable plaintiff. And this is where 'Jane Roe' entered the picture.

Weddington and Coffee were put in touch by Coffee's friend, Henry McClusky, a Dallas adoption lawyer and early gay rights activist, with a Norma Lea McCorvey (née Nelson). Twenty-one, divorced and already pregnant with her third child, she had led a traumatic short life. Born in Louisiana to parents of Cajun and Cherokee background, she was raised in

FIGURE 8.1. Sarah Weddington. Courtesy of the National Archives

Houston by her alcoholic and physically abusive mother as a Jehovah's Witness. When she was ten, she stole a small amount of money from a gas station and was banished to Mount St. Michaels, a harsh Catholic boarding school. In her teenage years, Norma was in and out of reform schools. Despite the hardships, she later asserted that this was nevertheless 'the happiest period in her life'. At 16, she married Woody McCorvey, an itinerant steel worker. She was abused by him and left one year later to live with her mother; she was pregnant. Her first daughter, Melissa, was born in 1965 and, against Norma's wishes, was taken into her mother's legal custody.

Norma quickly slipped into alcoholism and casual drug use. After coming out as a lesbian, she worked as a bartender in a gay bar in Dallas (The White Carriage) and as a carnival barker. At 19, she became pregnant again and gave the child up for adoption. Still struggling to get her life sorted out, she became pregnant for a third time when she was 21. As abortions were illegal in Texas, she wanted to go out-of-state, but was unable to pay for travel or an abortion. Her doctor put her in touch with Henry McClusky (who was to be shot to death in 1973 by a disaffected gay lover). Instead of arranging an adoption, McClusky introduced Norma to Linda Coffee and Sarah Weddingtion.

At five months pregnant, Norma met Coffee and Weddington in a local pizzeria. She agreed to become 'Jane Roe' and a class action was filed against Henry Wade, the Dallas district-attorney, on behalf of her and other Texan women; it was a direct challenge to the constitutionality of the Texas statute criminalising abortion. Wade was a strict law-and-order prosecutor who obtained death sentences in all but one of the thirty cases in which he asked for it; he had also been the lead prosecutor in Jack Ruby's trial, the murderer of Lee Harvey Oswald, President Kennedy's alleged killer. Norma's suit also sought an injunction against Wade that prevented him from further enforcing the statute against doctors who were the actual law-breakers, not the pregnant women. As things turned out, Norma had little involvement in the ensuing legal action; she gave birth to her third child before the Texas court heard the case and gave up the child for immediate adoption. With a certain tragic irony, the fact was that the Jane Roe herself never had an abortion nor the choice to have one.

In mounting this case in March 1970, Coffee and Weddington were by all indications way out of their depth. They were still in their twenties and had little litigation experience at all, let alone in the specialised world of constitutional challenges. Nevertheless, they were undaunted and, with the confidence that comes from being young and idealistic, set their sights on making it all the way to Washington and the Supreme Court. The odds, therefore, were very much stacked against them. This was not least of all because they had to confront both a constitutional law that was far from encouraging and a history of abortion and its legal regulation that was far from straightforward or supportive.

In the early days of the republic, abortion was relatively common and largely unregulated. The common law paid no heed to abortions if performed before 'quickening' (around 20 weeks or so when the woman begins to feel movement). Commercial concoctions were openly advertised and available, but too often proved to be dangerous and sometimes fatal to the women using them. As a result in the early and mid-1800s, some states intervened to ban various abortifacients in order to protect women's health. However, this benign intervention heralded broader-based efforts to control abortion. The American Medical Association (AMA) and Protestant moralists became unlikely allies in seeking to criminalise abortion. In different ways, they both acted of professional and religious self-interest; one to protect their professional turf and the other to advance their sectarian aspirations. By the turn of the century, abortion had been extensively criminalised; this did little to reduce the incidence of abortion (which was much higher than today as no reliable contraceptives yet existed) and did a lot to increase the death toll from back-street abortions. Women of privileged class were still able to terminate their pregnancies by travelling abroad or visiting private clinics.

By the 1960s, the tables were beginning to turn. Several forces were emerging to form a combined front against continued criminalisation. Ironically (in light of its earlier stance), the AMA recognised that abortion was inevitable and should be rendered safer and more regulated; the decision to terminate should be a medical matter, not a criminal issue. On another front, scientists began to caution against the threat of overpopulation. So developed was this push for decriminalisation that even the cautious American Law Institute (ALI) adopted in 1962 a model statute that allowed abortion to protect a woman's life or health, in cases of rape and where a child would be born with grave physical or mental defects. The United Kingdom also liberalised laws around abortion in the mid-1960s.

Yet the main impetus for change came from women themselves. As they gained greater sexual freedom and access to oral contraceptives, woman began to campaign for equality with men. This entailed obtaining full control over their own bodies; the availability of abortion was considered an integral component of women's entitlement to determine their own reproductive processes. Grassroots organisations in large cities began to provide support services and networks to enable women to obtain healthier, even if still illegal, abortions. What Weddington was involved in Texas was becoming commonplace across the United States. Of course, this led to a conservative and religious backlash. Led by Catholic groups and supported by evangelical movements, the anti-choice forces couched many of their moral arguments in secular terms in order to garner more broad-based political support. Nixon's Republican party exploited the issue for political gain and became the anti-abortion party as a way to attract Catholics and social conservatives away from the Democrats.

As Coffee and Weddington prepared to go to court in 1970, the legal terrain was varied and shifting. In 1967, Colorado, North Carolina and California passed liberalised abortion statutes based on the ALI model statute. Nine other states followed in the next three years. Moreover, in 1970, four states (Alaska, Hawaii, New York and Washington) repealed their abortion bans and allowed abortion without restrictions in the early stages of pregnancy. This liberalisation was matched to some extent by developments in constitutional law. The Supreme Court had decided in *Griswold v. Connecticut* in 1965 that the criminalisation of contraceptive sales violated married couples' right to privacy; this was extended in 1972 in *Eisenstaedt v. Baird* to unmarried people. Also, in 1971, Congress had repealed laws that criminalised the publication, distribution and possession of information on abortion or contraception.

The scene was set, therefore, for a mighty legal and constitutional battle as the social upheaval of the 1960s began to permeate governmental and political institutions and elites. The public mood had begun to shift and many opinion polls showed that support was growing for the idea that a woman's decision whether to terminate her pregnancy should be between her physician and herself; this increasing liberalisation cut across religious and political lines. The fact that abortion remained so unsafe still in 1965 – that 17 per cent of all deaths due to pregnancy and childbirth were the result of illegal abortions – was sufficient to overcome some people's moral and political qualms. Coffee and Weddington set about their task with enthusiastic indignation and youthful optimism. Win or lose, they intended to put the abortion issue front and centre in the national consciousness.

MRS WEDDINGTON GOES TO WASHINGTON

The *Roe v. Wade* action was first heard on 17 June 1970 in Dallas; it was joined by James Hallford, a licensed physician, who had been previously prosecuted and sought to challenge the Texas laws. The three-judge panel on the Federal District Court struck down the Texas abortion statutes. Relying on the concurring opinion of Justice Goldberg in the earlier *Griswold* decision of the Supreme Court, it held that the statutes were so vague and overbroad as to infringe the plaintiffs' Ninth Amendment right to privacy. However, the court did not grant an injunction against prosecution and Wade, as district-attorney, declared that he would continue to prosecute physicians that performed abortions. Both parties appealed and Coffee and Weddington got their hoped-for trip to Washington.

Weddington took the lead role in making arguments to the Supreme Court on 13 December 1971. Still only 26, she was obviously nervous. As she put it, 'I wanted to make a last stop before I went in, but there was no ladies room in the lawyers' lounge'. Her presentation did not go as well as she might have hoped. Considerable time was taken up in her allotted thirty minutes with tough questions from the justices about whether McCorvey had 'standing' – a personal stake in the controversy – to bring the constitutional challenge as she was no longer pregnant and as she, as the pregnant woman, was not subject to criminal prosecution. However, if her arguments seemed to fall short, those of her opposing counsel, Jay Floyd, the Assistant Attorney General, got off to an even worse start. In an ill-chosen opening, he repeated an old joke: 'When a man argues against two beautiful ladies like this, they are going to have the last word'. The bench greeted it with stunned silence.

Fortunately, for both sides, the Supreme Court requested reargument. There had been only seven justices present the first time around as Justices Hugo Black and John Harlan had very recently retired. When Justices Lewis Powell and William Rehnquist joined the Court in 1972, it was decided to rehear counsels' arguments. So, on 11 October 1972, Sarah Weddington got a chance to do a better job; this she did much to her and her supporters' relief. Her concern was less with convincing the judges of any particular constitutional theory about a woman's right to abortion and more with simply persuading the Supreme Court to constitutionalise it. On the other side, the hapless Jay Floyd was replaced by Robert Flowers, another member of the Dallas Attorney General's office. Although he improved on Floyd's performance, he came under strong fire from Justices Potter Stewart and Thurgood Marshall.

The decision of the Supreme Court was issued on 22 January 1973. By a 7–2 majority, it was held that the Texan laws should be struck down as being unconstitutional. Although such a significant decision received expected attention, it was overshadowed somewhat by the death of former President Lyndon B. Johnson on that same day. In fact, Weddington only found out that she had won the case when the *New York Times* called and asked if she had a comment on the decision: 'should she?' asked her assistant. Later that day, she received a telegram from the Clerk of the Supreme Court that stated 'JUDGEMENT ROE against WADE today affirmed in part and reversed in part. Opinions AIRMAILED'. Coffee and Weddington were thrilled. As was Norma McCorvey who, four days later, outed herself as 'Jane Roe' and expressed her pride at being involved in such a pathbreaking case.

Justice Harry Blackmun gave the opinion of the all-male Court. He was joined by Justices Warren Burger, William Douglas, William Brennan, Potter Stewart and Thurgood Marshall. After attending the same grade school in Minnesota as Chief Justice Burger, Blackmun was a Harvard Law School grad and an early member of its Glee club. He initially practiced law in a small firm, but later became counsel to the Mayo Clinic (a not-for-profit medical practice/research group) in the 1950s. He was a life-long Republican and was appointed to the Supreme Court in 1970 by Richard Nixon on the advice of Warren Burger, Blackmun's long-time friend. Indeed, in his early years on the Court, Blackmun earned the nickname, the Minnesota Twin, as he tended to side with the Chief Justice on most issues. However, he began to forge his own path and became an increasingly liberal judge as his long bench career progressed. Indeed, the decision in *Roe*, bearing in mind its timing and impact, may well have been his and the Court's most liberal and controversial decision of all time.

Although it is wrong-headed to draw any direct connections between it and his judgment in *Roe*, one of Blackmun's three daughters, Sally, had earlier had to sacrifice her university education due to an unplanned pregnancy; she later confessed that this was 'a decision that I might have made differently had *Roe v. Wade* been around'. Consequently, while Justice Blackmun acknowledged that 'one's philosophy, one's experiences, one's exposure to the raw edges of human existence, one's religious training, one's attitudes toward life and family and their values, and the moral standards one establishes and seeks to observe, are all likely to influence and to color one's thinking and conclusions about abortion', he insisted that the task of the court was 'to resolve the issue by constitutional measurement, free of emotion and of predilection'. Looking back over more than half a century's jurisprudence, the majority glimpsed a constitutional right that had previously been available, but largely unarticulated and unexplored – 'the right to privacy'.

Although the US Constitution does not explicitly mention any right to privacy at all, there was an established line of cases, including *Griswold* in 1965 and *Eisenstadt* in 1972, that had interpreted the Fourteenth Amendment so as to ground a fundamental entitlement to personal liberty from state interference. Moreover, according to Justice Blackmun, such a right encompasses a woman's decision whether or not to terminate her pregnancy. However, the Court decided that this right was not absolute and, as the pregnancy progresses, must be limited by or give way to the state's legitimate interest in protecting both the woman's health and the potential life that is involved. In short, the state's interests become more 'compelling' and eclipse the rights of the woman as she moves into the later stages of her pregnancy. Accordingly, the Court recommended a trimestered approach to the regulation of abortion by qualified medical practitioners:

With respect to the State's important and legitimate interest in the health of the mother, the 'compelling' point ... is at approximately the end of the first trimester. It follows that, from and after this point, a State may regulate the abortion procedure to the extent that the regulation reasonably relates to the preservation and protection of maternal health. Examples of permissible state regulation in this area are requirements as to the qualifications of the person who is to perform the abortion; as to the licensure of that person; as to the facility in which the procedure is to be performed, that is, whether it must be a hospital or may be a clinic or some other place of less-than-hospital status; as to the licensing of the facility; and the like. For the period of pregnancy prior to this 'compelling' point, the attending physician, in consultation with his patient, is free to determine, without regulation by the State, that, in his medical judgment, the patient's pregnancy should be terminated. If that decision is reached, the judgment may be effectuated by an abortion free of interference by the State.

Justice Byron 'Whizzer' White filed a resounding dissent. He was something of a renaissance figure. Not only was he a star academic and Rhodes Scholar, but he was also a celebrated rushing back for the NFL's Detroit Lions and was elected to the Football Hall of Fame. He gave the majority's decision short shrift by emphasising the Court's 'improvident and extravagant exercise of the power of judicial review'. He concluded that, while he 'might agree' with the Court's trimester scheme, it was for the people and state legislatures to determine the balance between a mother's decision to terminate and the protection of a future human life; judges had no business trampling into such morally and politically fraught territory.

Justice William Rehnquist joined White in dissent. A recent Nixon appointee who went on to become a long-serving Chief Justice from 1986 to 2005, Rehnquist was a conservative in both his politics and his judicial approach. While he conceded that a person's liberty embraces more than those rights specifically enumerated in the Constitution, he could not countenance the idea that it should extend to 'the Court's sweeping invalidation of any restrictions on abortion during the first trimester'. Condemning the majority's approach as 'judicial legislation', he rejected the idea that 'the conscious weighing of competing factors that the Court's opinion apparently substitutes for the established test' has no basis at all in 'the intent of the drafters of the Fourteenth Amendment'. In so doing, Rehnquist lit a constitutional and interpretive torch that has continued to burn strongly for more than forty years – 'originalism' as a source of constitutional meaning.

THE DEBATE THAT NEVER DIES

Looking back, the immediate response to the Supreme Court's decision seems decidedly contained in light of the present and continuing hullabaloo around *Roe*. However, not surprisingly, those who did speak out took extreme positions; there was shock on both sides. Supporters celebrated the 'extraordinary' decision and took the view that 'Jan. 22, 1973 will stand out as one of the great days for freedom and free choice'. Opponents, of course, took a much more condemnatory tone: a Catholic Cardinal opined that it was 'an unspeakable tragedy' and urged Americans to 'rededicate themselves to the protection of the sacredness of life'. Richard Nixon's White House fumed, but said little publicly. After all, the President had appointed three members of the majority; only Rehnquist had towed the Republican party line.

As a result of what was perceived as unruly judicial activism, there was simmering talk of a possible constitutional amendment being sought to remedy the situation. Nothing transpired. Indeed, the sense was that, whatever the rights and wrongs of the situation, the Supreme Court had brought the debate on abortion to a close in terms of its constitutional and institutional acceptance. Zealots might continue to fight on and seek retrenchment or further extension of a woman's right to choose, but the mainstream war was over. The intervening forty years has demonstrated how premature and wrong that assessment was. The battleground over abortion is more heated today than it has ever been.

Indeed, the opponents of Blackmun's opinion and abortion generally have been successful in orchestrating a campaign against *Roe* and have effectively mobilised massive popular support. A 'March for Life' protest has been held annually around the anniversary of *Roe* since 1974, although there was also a 'March for Women's Lives' of 800,000 women in Washington in 2004 in support of greater reproductive freedom for women. However, this expression of moral outrage against *Roe* has spilled over into extreme acts of violence and vigilantism, including bombings and shootings. In 1993, two doctors who performed abortions were shot in Florida and Kansas. Things got worse in 1994 when another Florida doctor was murdered by a former pastor, and two receptionists at Boston abortion clinics were killed by a rampaging gunman. And in 1997, two bombs at an Atlanta building injured six people and left an abortion clinic in ruins.

Many supporters of a woman's right to choose view the *Roe* decision with considerable ambivalence. On the one hand, they are grateful to the Supreme Court majority for striking down the Texan ban on abortions and for establishing some rudimentary right to choose; American society is adjudged to be a better society with rather than without *Roe*. On the other hand, others maintain that the victory in *Roe* was almost pyrrhic. So determined were Coffee and Weddington to win that they failed to place the hard-won right on solid and dependable analytical ground. Rather than base a woman's right to choose on privacy, it is contended that an argument under the Fourteenth Amendment's protection of equality would have been better able to withstand the legal and judicial deprivations that have since occurred. Indeed, Justice Ruth Ginsberg, a professed supporter of a woman's right to choose, questioned the constitutional and political wisdom of Blackmun's judgment in *Roe* which, in trying to do too much too quickly, likely sowed the seeds for its own instability as a legal precedent.

However, whatever the popular and moral acceptability of abortions now being legal, there was a marked improvement in the lives and health of women. The *Roe* decision had little effect on the number of abortions sought and performed, but the impact on women's health from the shift from it being an illegal and backstreet activity to it being a legal and medically supervised procedure was immense. Whereas, in 1965, abortion was so unsafe that 17 per cent of all deaths due to pregnancy and childbirth resulted from illegal abortions, it has now been reduced to less than 0.3 per cent of women sustaining a serious complication after a legal abortion. Nevertheless, this statistic has to be read against the fact that there has been a significant decline in the number of abortion providers in the United States; it fell from 2,908 in 1982 to 1,793 in 2008. Indeed, there are many areas in the Southern United States that have no providers at all: women who seek an abortion are obliged to travel to obtain one. Sadly, it is *deja vu* all over again – the ghost-like memory of a young pregnant Sarah Weddington still haunts large sections of American

FIGURE 8.2. Pro-choice protester at the U.S. Supreme Court in 2012.
Courtesy of HazteOir.org / Flickr

women. Once again, it is low-income, young, and minority
women that are most affected.

JUDICIAL WOBBLES

Although *Roe* has never been overturned, its effect and reach
have been severely compromised and eroded by legislative
initiatives. A woman's right to choose an abortion has been
hedged by creating more and more regulatory hurdles to

access – state and federal funding has been strictly controlled and reduced; parental consent has been required for young women; bans have been imposed on late-term abortions; and waiting periods have been mandated. These incursions and constraints have generally, but not entirely, been permitted by the Supreme Court. An early decision in *Harris v. MacRae* in 1980 set the tone by approving stiff restrictions on making federal funding available for abortions. As the composition of the Supreme Court has changed, the precedential force of *Roe* has weakened.

As early as 1989, in *Webster v. Reproductive Health Services*, the Supreme Court struck down a Washington law that declared that 'life begins at conception' and banned the use of public facilities for abortions as unconstitutional but did not explicitly reaffirm *Roe*. However, by 1992 in *Planned Parenthood v. Casey*, two members of the Court, William Rehnquist and Antonin Scalia, went so far as to insist that *Roe* was wrongly decided. Most recently, in 2007 in *Gonzales v. Carhart*, a conservative majority of five upheld the constitutionality of a federal law criminalising late-term abortions. While the justices did not go as far as overturning *Roe*, they did claim that the federal statute was consistent with *Roe* whether it was valid or not. As the dissenting four justices pointed out, such a decision effectively overruled a central feature of *Roe* that the Supreme Court had repeatedly emphasised: that women's health must be the paramount concern in any laws that seek to restrict abortion even after the first semester. As further changes to the Supreme Court's membership occur, *Roe* will come under further challenge.

As for the main players in the original *Roe* drama, they have each travelled different paths. Justice Blackmun's opinion has continued to be a target for both proponents and opponents of a woman's right to choose. In lectures and speeches, he championed women's equality and chastised its foes. His stance was crystallised in *Thornburgh* in 1986 when he opined that no decision is 'more personal and intimate ... or more basic to individual dignity and autonomy' than a woman's right to terminate her pregnancy. In return, he received hate mail and even death threats. Yet he never wavered in his support. When he retired from the Supreme Court in 1994, he continued to be an advocate for *Roe*. Shortly before his death in 1999, he became the first and only Supreme Court judge to play a judge in a movie, Steven Spielberg's slave saga, *Amistad*.

As for the lawyers, the defendant Henry Wade continued as a District Attorney of Dallas County from 1951 to 1987; he never lost a case in which he personally led the prosecution. On his retirement, he became counsel to a Dallas law firm. However, since then, the Dallas District Attorney's office under Wade has come under scrutiny for some of its tactics and evidence used in criminal cases and a number of convictions were overturned on the basis of DNA testing. Linda Coffee was the silent partner in *Roe*'s legal team; she dropped out of the public spotlight, had a relatively low-key career litigating sex and race discrimination cases and stopped practicing in 2006. Sarah Weddington followed a very different path.

Almost immediately after her triumph in *Roe*, Weddington began serving in the Texas legislature for the first of her three terms. She was the first woman to be appointed general counsel to the US Department of Agriculture in 1977; she was a special assistant to President Jimmy Carter from 1978 to 1981; and she lectured at the Texas Wesleyan University from 1981 to 1990. In 1993, she published a book on her experiences, titled *A Question of Choice*. Still active and a survivor of breast cancer, she was an adjunct professor at the University of Texas in Austin until 2012 and has received several honorary degrees from Southern universities, but not from her own university, Texas. She also founded the Weddington Center that promotes leadership among women and operates as a home base for her own work. Hers was a stellar career of pride and achievement, but nothing could top her opening act in *Roe*.

That leaves the rather tragic figure of 'Jane Roe' herself, Norma McCorvey. Like most litigants, she played little part in the Supreme Court hearing. But, at the time of *Roe*'s

FIGURE 8.3. Norma McCorvey speaking at the Dublin Rally for
Life in 2009. Courtesy of Debra Sweet / Flickr

judgment, she did express her pride in being part of such a
ground-breaking decision on women's rights. By the time of
the ruling in early 1973, she was in an established lesbian
relationship with Connie Gonzalez; the couple lived together
and did house cleaning to make ends meet. However, in line
with her troubled past, Norma seemed to chop and change as
different people attempted to appropriate her for their cause.
Soon after she published an autobiography, *I Am Roe*, in
1994, she became an evangelical Christian: she disavowed
her support for *Roe* and became a pro-life activist.
A Christian publisher published her second autobiography,
Won by Love, in 1997. In it, she explained that:

I was sitting in O.R.'s offices when I noticed a fetal development
poster. The progression was so obvious, the eyes were so sweet. It
hurt my heart, just looking at them. I ran outside and finally, it
dawned on me. 'Norma', I said to myself, 'They're right'. I had
worked with pregnant women for years. I had been through three
pregnancies and deliveries myself. I should have known. Yet something in that poster made me lose my breath. I kept seeing the picture
of that tiny, 10-week-old embryo, and I said to myself, that's a baby!

I felt crushed under the truth of this realization. I had to face up to the awful reality. Abortion wasn't about 'products of conception'.... It was about children being killed in their mother's wombs. All those years I was wrong. Signing that affidavit, I was wrong. Working in an abortion clinic, I was wrong.... It was so clear. Painfully clear.

Soon after, Norma converted to Catholicism and declaimed her identity as a lesbian. Although for a time she did receive money from pro-life organisations, she stopped doing so after a number of years. Yet she remained active as a campaigner. She petitioned the Supreme Court unsuccessfully in 2005 to have *Roe* overturned, she was arrested in 2009 for disrupting the Senate confirmation hearing of judicial nominee, Sonia Sotomayor, a declared supporter of *Roe*'s decision, and she took part in an anti-Obama commercial on his bid for reelection. As is plain, she has led an unsettled and perhaps harrowing life. Yet, on more or less notorious terms, she will always be primarily known as the irrepressible 'Jane Roe'.

CONCLUSION

There are no cases in American politics and jurisprudence that have continued to be as controversial as *Roe v. Wade*. While there are decisions (e.g., *Brown* in 1954 on desegregation and *Lawrence* in 2003 on gay rights) that have been divisive at the time of their release, none has had the legs and staying power as *Roe*. The debate over abortion remains as intense, polarising and entrenched today as ever. A recent American poll reported that 25 per cent believed that abortion is morally wrong and *Roe* should be overturned; 18 per cent that it is morally wrong, but *Roe* should not be overturned; and 42 per cent that it is not morally wrong and *Roe* should not be overturned. Against this backdrop, as the membership of the Supreme Court changes and abortion becomes almost a litmus test for future nominees, *Roe*'s constitutional fate will remain uncertain, even if its status as great case is assured.

9

PLAYING A DIFFERENT TUNE

Fairness in deal making

Many people believe that 'a deal is a deal'. If you promised to do something, you should be obliged to follow through on it whether you made a good or bad deal. This is a moralistic stand often held by those who do not suffer fools gladly: 'act in haste, repent at leisure'. The law has generally hewed to this stark principle. However, there have developed several excuses or justifications for deviating from its harsh formalistic imperative – duress, mistake, fraud and the like. Yet until recently, the common law has resisted the temptation to peek behind the surface–appearance of particular deal-making promises and evaluate the fairness or substance of the deal. Justice was considered best served by leaving people to work out for themselves what is fair and to agree only to contractual commitments that were in their own best interests.

In recent decades, the common law has begun to adopt a more progressive and interventionist stance. In line with other more socially-minded initiatives, the courts have been prepared to look to the substantive merits of deals and not merely their superficial form before enforcing ill-considered and restrictive deals. In particular, there has been a greater willingness to recognise that not all deal makers are on an equal footing and that modern commerce has strengthened the hand of corporations to exact terms and conditions that might place the average consumer or person in an oppressive bind.

Although there is still much disagreement on exactly when deals should be set aside because of their substantive content even when there is clear consent, the common law (reinforced by strong legislative enactments) has placed substantive fairness and 'unconscionability' closer to the heart of contract and commercial law. The courts' concern is no longer only with the fairness of the contract-formation process, but also with the fairness of the outcome.

FIGURE 9.1. The 1908 cover of the sheet music to *Take Me out to the Ball Game* by Albert Von Tilzer, published by the York Music Company of Tin Pan Alley.

The leading case is an English one from the late 1960s and 1970s when the social world was beginning to experience significant change and realignment. Fittingly, it involved the world of Tin Pan Alley where big business and musical innovation collided. Young musicians and composers were looking for a foothold in the burgeoning music scene; they often made hasty and imprudent deals with wily music publishers. As the old order was challenged by fresh voices and new interests, the circumstances were in place for some legal battles that would pressure the music business to sing a different tune. A young breed of savvier composers and players wanted their share of the financial action.

DOWN THE ALLEY

'Tin Pan Alley' was the title given to that part of Manhattan, New York City, where the music publishing business took root in the late nineteenth century and flourished until the 1960s. It was located around West 28th Street between Fifth and Sixth Avenue. The basic idea was that publishing companies hired in-house songwriters, like Irving Berlin and later Jerry Leiber and Mike Stoller. They paid them to produce songs for particular artists. In this way, the organisations, like Hill & Range and BMI (Broadcast Music, Inc.), managed to keep a stranglehold on music composition and publishing. This had the effect of making it very difficult for young and unconnected composers to get their music and songs published and into the hands of those artists who might perform them best. The companies acted as an effective and lucrative gatekeeper.

While music publishing and recording was a precarious and fickle market (of about 30,000 songs recorded each year only about 20 per cent received more than one play on radio stations), vast sums were still made. Most of those funds ended up in the coffers of a few controlling companies, not the artists or the composers. However, by the 1960s, rock music began to challenge not only earlier and more mainstream musical traditions, but the complacent business establishment that dominated the music industry. Young composers and

FIGURE 9.2. Plaque at Tin Pan Alley. Courtesy of Ben
Sutherland / Flickr

artists wanted to control their own fate and receive their fair
share of the larger amounts of money on offer. New offices
began to open and new entrepreneurs began to get a foot in
the door.

One of those new offices was at 1650 Broadway. With
cheaper rents and younger founders, businesses like Aldon
Music, under the leadership of the legendary Don Kirshner,
the 'Man with the Golden Ear', began to wrest control from
the older order; writers like Neil Sedaka ('Calendar Girl'),
Carole King ('Will You Love Me Tomorrow') and Barry
Mann ('You've Lost That Loving Feeling') were employed
and made companies rich. However, composers were paid
modest salaries and still largely denied the full benefits of their
work. The old order was giving way, but some of its less
savoury and exploitive practices carried on.

Into this shifting milieu came Aaron Schroeder. A Brooklyn
boy, he was already in his forties when the musical revolution
of the 1960s took hold. Although claiming that he never
learned to read music, he had began his stellar career as a
songwriter at Hill & Range Publishing where he had penned
more than seventeen hits for Elvis Presley (including 'It's Now

or Never', which he wrote with Wally Gold in less than thirty minutes) and occasional hits for Frank Sinatra, Perry Como, Nat King Cole and Roy Orbison. In all, he wrote over 200 published songs in this period. But after a bitter legal feud with Presley's management in 1962, he began to turn his attention to the business side of the music publishing industry. And, as with his efforts at composing, he was extremely successful.

Renowned for his especially antagonistic posture in a business that was already renown for its aggressive approach, Schroeder bought January Music from the evergreen Dick Clark in 1964 and started his own label, Musicor. Although he had a great capacity to identify and attract emerging stars, he did not treat them well; his focus was always on the size of the bottom line rather than the quality of the music produced.

FIGURE 9.3. A Musicor Records release, 1973.
Courtesy of Sean O'Sullivan / Flickr

He benefitted from and then fell out with Hal David and Burt Bacharach when they wanted a fair shake. In a spectacular example, he helped nurture the iconoclastic talent of Jimi Hendrix and published his second album, 'Axis: Bold As Love', but paid him peanuts for the copyright to his compositions; this was as little as a couple of $100s in some cases.

With smart business instincts, Schroeder recognised that the fulcrum of music publishing was moving from New York and the United States to London and England. By 1965, he had sold off his American interests to United Artists and had started off new businesses in the United Kingdom. His main vehicle was the A. Schroeder Music Publishing Co. Ltd. that was situated on Essex Street in London's West End. Along with his wife, Abby, he was the sole shareholder and director. In characteristic style, he sought out aspiring songwriters and tied them to long-term contracts. It proved to be a reliable and rewarding enterprise.

One of those songwriters was Tony Macaulay. His real name was Anthony Instone and he was a London boy. In his teens, he had got his foot in the music door by acting as a record plugger. But he had an untutored knack for writing catchy music. Over a short span, he composed, often with John MacLeod, a clutch of chart-topping hit songs (the Foundations' 'Baby, Now That I Found You' and Edison Lighthouse's 'Love Grows Where My Rosemary Goes') on both sides of the Atlantic. Indeed, by the 1970s, he had been labelled as one of the three men, along with Roger Cook and Roger Greenaway, 'who ruled the London pop music world'. In his career, his songs sold more than 50 million records and he had 38 Top 20 hits. However, as a relative unknown and inexperienced 21-year-old, he had signed a publishing contract in July 1966 with Schroeder's company, although his larger ambition was to get into record production. And it is this fateful step that gave Macaulay legal notoriety as well as musical acclaim.

Although Macaulay hoped to negotiate a different set of terms and conditions, the agreement made was a standard form one that Schroeder had utilised and developed over a number of years: it was not untypical for the music industry generally. It was presented as a take-it-or-leave-it deal. The basic nature of the contract was that, over a five-year term, Macaulay would give to Schroeder the full copyright to each musical composition in return for standard royalties of a varying rate between 5 and 50 per cent of sales made. However, there were several specific terms that gave particular colour to the contract:

(a) Although Schroeder received copyright over all Macaulay's present and future work, he was not under any obligation to publish any of that music;

(b) Schroeder could terminate the Agreement by giving one month's notice, but Macaulay had no corresponding right to do so;

(c) If Macaulay's royalties exceeded £5,000, the Agreement would be automatically extended for a further five years;

(d) Macaulay was only entitled to a payment of £50 for his compositions until he earned that amount in royalties; and

(e) Although Schroeder could transfer the agreement to any other person without Macaulay's permission, Macaulay had no corresponding right to do so.

As Macaulay became more successful, he began to have serious and obvious doubts about the fairness and reasonableness of this arrangement. In particular, he rankled at the length of the agreement and the imbalance of rights and entitlements; it was all to Schroeder's advantage at the expense of his own. When the agreement had automatically been renewed for a further five years as a result of the songs' successes, Macaulay decided to consult lawyers. He was told that, despite the common law's traditional reluctance to look to the substantive merits of contracts, it was well worth a shot at challenging the agreement as being contrary to public policy, a 'restraint of trade' and thereby of no force and effect. Moreover, it was suggested that Macaulay might claim that the agreement had been repudiated as a result of Schroeder's dealings around foreign sales. However, it is the unconscion-ability claim that occupied the courts and went on to become a path-breaking precedent in the law of contract.

THROUGH THE COURTS

After the usual extended period of procedural wrangling and postured negotiations, the case was unresolved and came on for trial in the Chancery Division of the High Court in late July 1972. By now, Macaulay had garnered greater success and further acclaim; this meant that he was a money-making machine for Schroeder. The stakes were per-sonally high for both Macaulay, the plaintiff, and Schroe-der, the defendant. But they also each served as champions for competing sides of the music publishing industry. In response to Macaulay's claim, Schroeder had also brought a counter-claim to seek an order by the court to have the contract performed.

The judge was Justice Plowman who was something of an old hand in handling such disputes as he had been involved in copyright litigation over Dylan Thomas's *Under Milk Wood* and John Lennon and Paul McCartney's songs. He found for the plaintiff, Macaulay. The basis for the decision was two-fold: that the contract was so restrictive of Macaulay's cap-acity to profit from his compositions that it was against public policy; and that there was behaviour by Schroeder that could be reasonably taken by Macaulay to amount to a repudiation of the contract. He ordered that the contract should be declared void and of no continuing effect. Macaulay was free to pursue whatever other avenues and agreements with others that he wished.

Schroeder wasted no time and appealed to the Court of Appeal. The case was heard a year later for a few days at the end of June and early July. Supported by Lord Justices Cairns and Goulding, Lord Justice Russell gave the judgment of the court. He was a war hero, receiving the French *Crois de Guerre* for bravery, and was from an Irish Catholic family of established legal standing. A talented and esteemed lawyer and judge in his own right, he was later appointed to the House of Lords where he became Lord Russell of Killowen (in Northern Ireland) and sat for seven years.

In this case, Russell laid down the general principle that contracts for personal service could be against the public interest and that it was for the defendant to demonstrate that any restrictions were reasonable. He went on to hold that the particular conditions placed on Macaulay were unreasonable as not only was Macaulay disadvantaged under the contract (i.e., no right to withdraw or transfer his rights), but Schroeder had no counter-balancing limitations placed on his actions (i.e., no obligation to publish Macaulay's work and could, therefore, pay a maximum of £50 to Macaulay if he chose). Moreover, Russell was of the opinion that, even if the restrictions had a superficial reasonableness, they were undermined by the excessive length of the contract and the unilateral terms for its extension.

Leave was obtained to appeal the case to the House of Lords as the issue was deemed to be of general public importance. The case was heard a year later on 15 and 16 July 1974. The lead counsel were experienced and highly regarded. Macaulay was represented by Robert Gatehouse who went on to become a High Court judge. A modest and likeable man, he was accomplished in many fields – a respectable jazz pianist, a gifted cartoonist, and an able wood sculptor. On the other side for Schroeder was Stephen Tumim who, while not as diverse in his talents as Gatehouse, was a social activist; he campaigned for the rights of deaf children (as he had two deaf daughters) and he played a central role in the reform of Britain's prisons in the 1980s and 1990s. Together, they ensured that all the main arguments were before the law lords as they reflected upon their decision.

The House of Lords handed down its reserved decision three months later on 16 October 1974. The bench consisted of some of the judicial heavy-hitters of the time – Lords Dilhorne, Diplock, Simon, Kilbrandon and Reid. The leading opinion was given by Lord Reid, the senior law lord, and was accompanied by strong concurring dicta from Lord Diplock.

Lord Reid of Drem was a candidate for inclusion in any British Hall of Judicial Fame. A Scot and long-time Unionist (Conservative) MP, he served as Scottish Solicitor General and Lord Advocate from 1941 to 1945. Unusually, he was appointed directly to the House of Lords in 1948 by Clement Attlee, the Labour PM, and served for a still unbeaten twenty-six years until 1974. As well as battling reactionary legal traditions (e.g., the continuation of a strict doctrine of precedent), James Reid was a red Tory and was sensitive to the plight of the underdog. For a civil lawyer, his opinion in *Macaulay v. Schroeder* was to become one of the enduring legacies of the common law.

Lord Reid was adamant that, where the terms of an agreement were self-evidently restrictive for one party, they must be justified by the other party who relies upon them. The gist of this burden was to demonstrate that 'the restrictions were no more than what was reasonably required to protect … legitimate interests'. Alighting on the salient fact that Schroeder was under no obligation at all to publish Macaulay's songs (and could simply let them gather dust in a drawer), he took the view that this was an entirely unreasonable restraint on Macaulay's right to publish and profit from his own work. Refraining from laying down any grand principle of contractual equity, Lord Reid took a measured and modest stance:

I do not find any evidence in this case, nor does it seem probable, that this form of contract made between a publisher and unknown composer has been molded by any pressure of negotiation. Any contract by which a person engages to give his exclusive services to another for a period necessarily involves extensive restrictions during that period of the common law right to exercise lawful activity he chooses in such a manner as he thinks best. Normally the doctrine of restraint of trade has no application to such restrictions; they require no justification. But if contractual restrictions appear to be unnecessary or to be reasonably capable of enforcement in an oppressive manner, then they must be justified before they can be enforced.

Lord Diplock of Wansford added his own particular emphasis to these reasons. A little tetchy and academic in demeanour, he was respected, if not liked by lawyers and colleagues; he did not suffer fools gladly. As a no-nonsense judge, he played a leading role in setting up special tribunals and procedures for dealing with terrorism in Northern Ireland a couple of years earlier in 1972. However, Kenneth Diplock was the son of a solicitor and he had a stellar legal career at the commercial bar, becoming a King's Counsel at the relatively young age of 41. He was well-suited to wade into the topical debate about the fairness of commercial contracts.

Lord Diplock insisted that the key issue was one of fairness and that there must be a balance of benefits and burdens for both parties. In this case, he easily concluded that there was not: because where one side can adopt a take-it-or-leave attitude, there is 'a classic instance of superior bargaining power'. To reach this conclusion, he argued that juridical task was 'to assess the relative bargaining power of the publisher and the song-writer at the time the contract was made and to decide whether the publisher had used his superior bargaining power to exact from the song-writer promises that were unfairly onerous to him'. Drawing an important distinction between standard-form contracts that were the products of good faith negotiations over time and those between parties who were in very different relative positions of power (as here), Diplock held that:

[The terms and conditions of the contract] have been dictated by that party whose bargaining power, either exercised alone or in conjunction with other providing similar goods or services, enables him to say: 'If you want these goods or services at all, these are the only terms on which they are obtainable. Take it or leave it in'.

Together, these statements took the common law of contracts forward in a new direction. No longer was the fact that the formal requirements for contract formation had been met sufficient alone to validate almost any substantive content of the contract. A more general notion of 'commercial fairness' was introduced. Of course, as is the way of the common law, the House of Lord's judgments left many questions unanswered; the task would be for later judges to fill out and elaborate upon the precise operation of this new category for challenging the enforceability of contracts. As is so often the case, commentators and judges had varying appetites for fulfilling this task. And the results were expectedly mixed.

EQUAL TO WHAT?

Of course, the courts had always refused to enforce certain kinds of contracts (e.g., slavery and prostitution) as offending public policy. However, *Macaualay*'s judgments had the potential to go much further. Although the House of Lords' introduction of 'unconscionability' received general approval as recognising an indubitable fact of modern society (i.e., that bargaining did not always – or hardly ever – occur on a level playing-field), there was consternation about how this potentially wide-ranging doctrine might operate. Some were antagonistic to paternalistic efforts to interfere with the operation of the market; they felt that, all things considered, such judicial tinkering was likely to lead to more, not less, confusion and uncertainty. Others were troubled that this liberal intervention might be wielded in too conservative a manner; they worried that the occasional striking down of a few contracts might serve to validate the bulk of other contracts in a market where there existed systemic and almost incorrigible inequality.

Indeed, almost all commentators seemed to agree that the concept's essentially protean nature was to be disparaged; there needed to be a clearer and more compelling statement of unconscionability's sweep and force. And the courts were not slow to oblige. In particular, judges made it clear that it was not simply the existence of the parties' unequal bargaining position that would render contracts unenforceable. Instead, judges were at pains to emphasise that it was the abuse of that position that was necessary. An inquiry would need to be made in each case as to whether a party had used its superior bargaining power unfairly and whether the allegedly oppressed party had meaningful contractual alternatives available and the opportunity to negotiate better terms and conditions in a competitive marketplace.

For the music industry, this was a 'watershed' decision. In a number of cases involving the music recording industry over the next decade, the English Court of Appeal affirmed both the letter and spirit of *Macaulay* and refused to enforce contracts that were much less oppressive than in that case. For instance, in the *Clifford Davis Management* case that was decided only a few days after the decision in *Macaulay*, it was held that, when a manager or publisher uses a standard-form contract to drive an unconscionable bargain, they must ensure that the artist (in this case, 'Fleetwood Mac') received independent legal advice. However, while the availability of independent legal advice became important, its existence did not prevent some judges from still setting aside contracts if their terms were sufficiently onerous and one-sided.

However, perhaps the high-point of 'unconscionability' came a year later in 1975. This was the memorable case of *Lloyd Bank v. Bundy* and featured the irrepressible Lord Denning. Herbert Bundy was a farmer and a fond father. He guaranteed a loan from the bank to his son's floundering company by way of a charge against his only asset, his farmhouse home. As the company got into further difficulties, Herbert increased his indebtedness to the bank. However, the bank had not been entirely forthright with the legally unrepresented Herbert and had failed to reveal the full extent of his son's company's problems. When the company went under, the bank foreclosed on the farmhouse and left Herbert almost destitute (and in poor health as he suffered a heart-attack while giving evidence at trial).

In a characteristically sweeping judgment, Lord Denning took the bank to task and held that, because it was in a vastly superior bargaining position to the gauche and inexperienced farmer, it was incumbent on them to take a more generous and less laissez-faire approach. While the common law would not interfere in most contractual arrangements, it would in circumstances where there was a stark inequality of bargaining power and undue pressure or unfair advantage had been taken: 'where the parties have not met on equal terms – when the one is so strong in bargaining power and the other so weak – that, as a matter of common fairness, it is not right that the strong should be allowed to push the weak to the wall'. Denning went on to craft a general principle that sought to bring coherence and analytical force to contract law:

The English law gives relief to one who, without independent advice, enters into a contract upon terms which are very unfair . . ., when his bargaining power is grievously impaired by reason of his own needs or desires, or by his own ignorance or infirmity, coupled with undue influences or pressures brought to bear on him by or for the benefit of the other. I do not mean to suggest that the principle depends on any wrongdoing. The one who stipulates for an advantage may be moved solely by self-interest, unconscious of the distress he is bringing to the other. . . . One who is in extreme need may knowingly consent to a most improvident bargain, solely to relieve the straits in which he finds himself.

Since 1985, lawyers and judges have not been entirely welcoming to Denning's efforts. Realising the broad and political import of his stance, they have sought to cabin its wide and open range of application. Indeed, in the following decade, the House of Lords, especially in the opinions of Lord Scarman, refused to adopt Denning's principled approach. Instead, it took a more circumspect and pragmatic stance in which they sought to find more than 'the unfair use of a dominant bargaining position' before setting aside contracts; there needed to be some element of wrongdoing. Indeed, in *Westminster Bank v. Morgan* in 1985 (on not dissimilar facts to *Bundy*), the House of Lords held that the relationship between banker and customer is not one that ordinarily gives rise to a presumption of undue influence; there needed to be specific and special proof that the bank had used its superior knowledge and power to the customer's disadvantage.

Today, the court's willingness to go beyond inquiries into the fairness of the contract-formation process is restrained. Judges have been wary about turning the law of contracts into an open-ended evaluation of the substantive fairness of contracts; the number of cases in which contracts have been set aside are few and far between. Nevertheless, reinforced by the advent of more progressive consumer legislation, the real world of contractual negotiation has been beneficially impacted by the flurry of cases in the 1970s and 1980s. Whatever its deficiencies, the doctrine of unequal bargaining power highlighted the pervasive problem of economic and social disparities in bargaining power, even if it inevitably dealt with its symptoms, not its sources. Consequently, however imperfectly, legal doctrine has at least given weaker parties one small weapon to challenge the status quo.

CONCLUSION

The impact of *Macaulay v. Schroeder* on the music business was not insignificant. There is some credibility to Tony Macaulay's own assessment that 'music publishing is a kinder, more equitable business than that of old' because of the case. Whether that was brought about by dint of the legal decision alone is debatable. Even great cases can only hope to change the law; they rarely have an easy or direct effect on society and its economic relations. That is a much more murky and speculative venture.

As for the main players in the legal drama, they both managed to go on and have very successful lives. Aaron Schroeder stayed in England for a substantial amount of time; he and his wife organised celebrity concerts and helped to establish the Berkshire Theatre Festival. Having amassed considerable wealth from his over 1,500 published songs, he lived until 2009 and died at age 83 after a lengthy illness and spell in the Lillian Booth Actors' Home in Englewood, California. Although cast as the almost vaudevillian villain of the legal piece, Schroeder's musical contributions did bring great pleasure to many millions. The shame is that his aggressive business approach tended to overshadow his undoubted musical talents.

By the time that his lawsuit was finally resolved, Tony Macaulay had achieved great success as a pop music composer. However, he walked away from the pop music business and began to explore musical theatre and movies; his songs had legs, and they were featured in the movies *There's Something About Mary* (1998) and *Shallow Hal* (2001). He is also the nine-time winner of the coveted Ivor Novello Award and is the only Brit to have received the Edwin Forrest Award for contributions to the American theatre. In 1986, he was chosen to write the music to commemorate the Queen's 60th Birthday celebrations; it was performed by a choir of 600 children and the Grenadier Guards outside Buckingham Palace. As if all this was not enough, he has also had another career as a thriller writer. In the 1990s, he published *Sayonara* and *Enemy of The State* to some critical acclaim; he teaches a course on thriller writing at the University of Brighton. Against all this, Tony Macaulay's triumph in the courts seems a relatively small feather in his ample cap.

10

CONCLUSION

Surfing the tides

As all these great cases attest, the development of the common law is a game of chance. It is difficult to predict their *when, where* and *why*. They sometimes appear from nowhere or, at least, the most unlikely of circumstances. But they go on, for whatever reason, to have a momentous effect on the future orientation and development of the law. Some stand the test of time and the effects of future tinkering; others have lead a charmed if relatively short life and are replaced by a new case on the block. The common law manages to survive and perhaps strengthen itself by these both fatal and life-affirming acts of transformation.

Efforts to explain the dynamics and drama of change are manifold. A variety of metaphors have been used to demonstrate that not only is change inevitable, but also that such change is manageable and limited. A favourite one goes back to the infamous *Edwards* case in 1929, when Lord Sankey of the Privy Council chastised the Supreme Court of Canada for its unwillingness to interpret 'persons' as including women, whatever the meaning of the term on its enactment fifty years earlier. In a delightful phrase, he compared the Constitution to 'a living tree capable of growth and expansion within its natural limits'. This metaphor has been applied generally to the common law at large. Recently, the Supreme Court of Canada has itself insisted that law is 'a living tree which, by way of progressive interpretation, accommodates and addresses the realities of modern life'.

While this metaphor does much to inform a more beneficial way of thinking about the common law, it is too narrow and restrictive in its reach. On the plus side, it makes clear that the law is organic, not ossified; it must develop and change if it is to flourish, not wither. This is no small acknowledgement that has managed to wrest the common law from the stranglehold of a more conservative and less expansive vision of law and law making. However, on the negative side, it unduly constricts the imagination. First, it depicts the common law as one organic entity, a tree. This misrepresents the fact that, as the history of great cases shows, the law can be one thing one day (e.g., a tree) and another thing another day (e.g., a bear). The judicial custodians of the common law process are not inhibited in their capacity to shift among species and even genera. At their best, they do this as if it is the most 'natural' move in the world.

Secondly and more problematically, Lord Sankey's description misleads in its efforts to suggest that there is some natural pattern or preordained pathway to the common law's future development. Indeed, the idea of 'progress' in both the natural and legal worlds seems a little far-fetched. There is, of course, some degree of progress in the law in that puzzles will be solved, rules will be refined, and principles will be honed. As the history of almost all great cases shows, the court makes a breakthrough decision and then sculpts out the more detailed contours of the new rule over an extended period. For instance, having established the general concept of 'unconscionability' in contract law, the courts have worked to determine in what circumstances contracts will be varied or set aside (Chapter 9) Again, having introduced the 'remoteness' principle into tort law, the courts have busied themselves with demarcating the scope and limits of that principle (Chapter 3). In both situations, however, it should be clear that any progress is contained and episodic. Furthermore, while the development of such doctrinal details may appear to be technical and uncontroversial, their elaboration is as political as the initial decision that made the original breakthrough, albeit of a more modest and focused nature (Chapter 8)

Consequently, it is true that while the law grows and thrives, it does not do so in a haphazard, capricious or arbitrary manner. Yet this does not mean that its limits are 'natural' in the sense of being somehow objective or separate from the predilections of its judicial cultivators or the influences of its changing social climate. The common law responds to the prevailing social mores through the selective interventions of judges; there is no natural way to proceed that stands entirely or largely aside from those tasked with tending it or from the informing context in which they find themselves. Indeed, the origins and lives of great cases confirm this insight.

As social climates change and judicial gardeners come and go, the status and appeal of different species changes too. There are few legal equivalents to the old-stand forests of Redwood. Although *Marbury* may be said to have withstood the test of time, this is as much to do with its constant tending, pruning and revitalisation as anything else (Chapter 4). In contrast, *Roe* has managed to survive for fifty years, but only in a much more truncated and cut-back form; judicial gardeners have succumbed to the social pressures to prune back its more expansive flowering, almost killing it in the process (Chapter 8). Similarly, *Macaulay* remains a part of the common law's garden, but its propensity to propagate widely has been held in check by a less than sympathetic judiciary (Chapter 9). So any talk of the common law's 'natural limits' must be tempered by the important (and some would say decisive) role that judges have in cultivating the organic process that is the common law.

In trying to explain the relation between judicial action and social mores, perhaps a more illuminating (if also limiting) way of grasping the common law process is to think about judges as surfers. In calm seas, judges can more effectively spot the prevailing social tides and, without much difficulty, ride the incoming breakers (Chapter 9). However, as the social seas become more roiled, the judges will need to exhibit greater perception and dexterity to spot and ride the turbulent whitecaps (Chapter 2). The gnarly currents may well be competing with each other and the swells may run dangerously high (Chapter 8). In such seas, the task of the judge will be fraught with risk, but the challenges and the meeting of them will be so much more exciting. On occasion, a judge will manage to surf in on the most demanding of tides. But at other times, they might simply wipe out or be pitched over (Chapters 3 and 7).

In short, to be a good surfer is much like being a good judge – you need to be able to read the currents as much as ride them (Chapter 6). The good judge will need to be attentive to the complex swell of social views, time it right and chart a safe path through their confusing waters (Chapter 5). But the best of judges – the Duke Kahanamokus of the bench – will carve out their own niche; they will do so with a distinctive style and brio that works against all odds in the most tempestuous of seas. As I have tried to show, great cases can be seen, time and time again, to arise from the efforts of judges, great and good, to catch a wave and 'rip'; they see and do what eludes others. That takes imagination, instinct, talent and the courage to get it wrong.

SOURCES

Chapter 1

Burns, R. 'Let Not Woman E'er Complain', in *Poetical Works of Robert Burns*, 435 (W. Wallace ed., 1902).

Donne, J. 'The Nursery of Music, Joy Life and Eternity: Elegie III ll.35–36', in *The Complete Poetry and Selected Prose of John Donne*, 59 (C. Coffin, ed., 2001).

Douglas, William. 'Stare Decisis' (1949) 49 *Colum. L. Rev.*, 735.

Herschel, J., qtd. in Darwin, 'Letter to Charles Lyell, December 10, 1859', in *Charles Darwin's Letters: A Selection 1825–1859*, 208 (F. Burkhardt, ed., 1996).

Hutchinson, Allan C. *Evolution and the Common Law* (2005).

Is Eating People Wrong?: Great Legal Cases and How They Shaped the World (2010).

Simpson, A. W. B. 'The Common Law and Legal Theory', in *Oxford Essays in Jurisprudence*, 91 (A. W. B. Simpson, ed., 1973).

Watkins v. Olafson, [1989] 2 SCR 750 at 760–761, per McLachlin J.

Zimmer, Carl. *Evolution: The Triumph of an Idea*, 135 (2001).

Chapter 2

Airedale NHS Trust v. Bland (1993), 1 All E.R. 821.

Cruzan v. Missouri Dept of Health (1990), 497 US 261.

Cuthbertson v. Rasouli (2013), 3 SCR 341.

Re M. W. v. M. and others (2011), EWHC 2443.

Scraton, Phil. *Hillsborough: The Truth* (2000).

'Terri Schiavo case', *Wikipedia*, http://en.wikipedia.org/wiki/Terri_Schiavo_case.

'Tony Bland', *Wikipedia*, http://en.wikipedia.org/wiki/Tony_Bland.

Chapter 3

Balmain Association, http://balmainassociation.org.au/news.php.

Barnard, Alan. 'Mort, Thomas Sutcliffe (1816–1878)', *Australian Dictionary of Biography*, http://adb.anu.edu.au/biography/mort-thomas-sutcliffe-4258.

Goodhart, Arthur L. 'The Brief Life Story of the Direct Consequence Rule in English Tort Law' (1967) 4 *Va. L Rev*, 857.

Hughes v. Lord Advocate (1963), AC 837.

Mort's Dock & Engineering Co. Ltd. v. Overseas Tankship (UK) Ltd., [1961] AC 388.

Mustapha v. Culligan of Canada Ltd., [2008] 2 SCR 114.

Overseas Tankship (UK) v. The Miller Steamship Co., [1966] 1 All ER 709 (PC).

Palsgraf v. Long Island R.R. (1928).

Polemis v. Furness Withy & Co., [1921] 3 KB 560.

Smith v. Leech Brain & Co. Ltd., [1962] 2 QB 405.

Lord Wright, 'Re Polemis' (1951) 14 *Modern Law Review*, 393.

Chapter 4

Corwin, Edward S. *The Doctrine of Judicial Review: Its Legal and Historical Basis and Other Essays* (Princeton: Princeton University Press, 2011).

Hamilton, Alexander. *The Federalist Papers* (Library of Congress, 1787–88), http://thomas.loc.gov/home/histdox/fed_78.html.

Konefsky, Samuel Joseph. *John Marshall and Alexander Hamilton: Architects of the Constitution* (New York: MacMillan, 1964).

Lochner v. United States (1905), 198 U.S. 45.

Mace, George and Albert P. Melone. *Judicial Review and American Democracy* (Ames, IA: Iowa State University Press, 1988).

Marbury v. Madison (1803), 5 U.S. 137.

Swindler, William F. *The Constitution and Chief Justice Marshall*, (New York: Dodd, Mead & Company, 1978).

Tushnet, Mark (ed.), *Arguing Marbury v. Madison* (Stanford: Stanford University Press, 2005).

The United States Judiciary Act of 1789 (ch. 20, 1 Stat. 73), http://memory.loc.gov/cgi-bin/ampage?collId=llsl&fileName=001/llsl001.db&recNum=196.

Chapter 5

Adams v. Cape Industries plc, [1990] Ch. 433 (A.C.).

Broderip v. Salomon, [1895] 2 Ch. 323.

Ireland, Paddy. 'The Triumph of the Company Legal Form, 1856–1914', in J. Adams, *Essays for Clive Schmitthoff* 58 (1983).

Friedman, Milton. 'The Social Responsibility of Business is to Increase Its Profits', *New York Times Magazine* (13 September 1970), www-rohan.sdsu.edulfaculty/dunnweb/rpmts.fried man .html.

Hutchinson, Allan C. *The Companies We Keep* (2005).

Hutchinson, Allan and Ian Langlois. 'Salomon Redux: The Moralities of Business' (2012) 35 *Seattle University Law Review,* 1109.

Hadden, Tom. *Company Law And Capitalism 3–36* (2nd edn. 1977).

Horwitz, Morton J. *The Transformation of American Law, 1780–1860* (1977).

In re Raphael, [1898] 1 Ch. 853.

Micklethwait, John and Adrian Wooldridge, *The Company: A Short History of a Revolutionary Idea 51–52* (2003).

Parkinson, John, Andrew Gamble and Gavin Kelly. (eds.). *The Political Economy of the Company* (2000).

R. v. Arnaud (1846), 9 QB 806.

Salomon v. A. Salomon & Co., [1897] A.C. 22 (H.L.).

de Tocqueville, Alexis. *Journeys to England and Ireland,* 108 (New York: Transaction Publishers 1979, 1835).

Trustees of Dartmouth College v. Woodward (1819), 17 U.S. 518 at 636.

Chapter 6

Cowan, Sharon. 'The Pain of Pleasure: Consent and the Criminalisation of Sado-Masochistic "Assaults"', in James Chalmers, Fiona Leverick and Lindsay Farmer, *Essays in Criminal Law in Honour of Sir Gerald Gordon,* Vol. 5 (2010).

Chandra-Shekeran, Sangeetha. *Theorizing the Limits of the 'Sadomasochistic Homosexual' Identity in R v. Brown* (Melbourne University LR, 1997).

English Law Reform Commission. *Criminal Law: Consent and Offences Against the Person, A Consultation Paper* (Consultation Paper No 134, 1994).

R v. Brown, [1994] 1 AC 212.

R v. Dica, [2004] 2 ALL ER 593.

R v. Donovan, [1934] 2 KB 498.

R v. Emmett (unreported, 18 June 1999), at para 45 in Dica decision http://bailii.org/ew/cases/EWCA/Crim/2004/1103.html.

R v. Wilson, [1997] QB 47.

Spanner Trust. www.spannertrust.org.

Chapter 7

Lord Bolingbroke, *On the Study and Use of History,* Letter 5 (1739).

Cooper, Austin. 'The Ken Murray Case: Defence Counsel's Dilemma' (2009) 47 *Criminal Law Quarterly,* 41.

Clemmer, Christopher. 'Obstructing the Bernardo Investigation: Kenneth Murray and the Defence Counsel's Conflicting Obligations to Clients and the Court' (2014) 1.2 *Osgoode Hall Review of Law and Policy*, 137.

Freedman, Monroe H. 'Perjury: The Lawyer's Trilemma' (1975) 1:1 *Litigation*, 26.

Giannarelli v. Wraith (1988), 165 CLR 543.

Meredith (1981), 29 Cal. 3d 682.

People v. Belge (1975), 83 Misc. 2d 186.

Proulx, Michel and David Layton. *Ethics and Canadian Criminal Law* (2001).

R. v. Murray (2000), 48 OR (3d) 544; 186 DLR (4th) 124; 144 CCC (3d) 289; 34 CR (5th) 290; [2000] OJ No 2182 (SCJ).

State Ex. Rel. Sowers v. Olwell (1964), 394 P.2d 681.

Williams, Stephen. *Karla: A Pact with the Devil* (2003).

Chapter 8

Brooks, David. 'Op-Ed., Roe's Birth, and Death', *New York Times* (21 April 2005), A23.

Brown v. Board of Education (1954), 347 US 483.

C-SPAN. 'Justice Blackmun on *Roe v. Wade* (June 20, 1995)', www.c-span.org/video/?183168-1/justice-blackmun-roe-v-wade.

Casey v. Planned Parenthood (1992), 505 US 833.

Garrow, David J. 'She Put the v in Roe v. Wade', *New York Times* (27 September 1992).

Greenhouse, Linda and Reva B. Siegel. 'Before (and After) Roe v. Wade: New Questions About Backlash' (2011) 120 *Yale L.J.*, 2028.

Kaplan, Laura. *The Story of Jane: The Legendary Underground Feminist Abortion Service* (University of Chicago Press, 1995)

Lawrence v. Texas (2003), 539 US 558.

McCorvey, Norma L. and Andy Meisler, *I Am Roe: My Life, Roe v. Wade and Freedom of Choice* (1994).

National Abortion Federation. 'History of Abortion', www.prochoice.org/about_abortion/history_abortion.html.

Pew Research. 'Public Opinion on Abortion and Roe v. Wade' (22 January 2013), www.pewforum.org/2013/01/22/public-opinion-on-abortion-and-roe-v-wade/.

Pollitt, Katha. 'Abortion in American History', *The Atlantic Monthly* (May 1997), www.theatlantic.com/past/docs/issues/97may/abortion.htm

Prager, Joshua. 'The Accidental Activist', *Vanity Fair* (February 2013), www.vanityfair.com/culture/2013/02/norma-mccorvey-roe-v-wade-abortion.

Reagan, Leslie J. *When Abortion Was a Crime: Women, Medicine, and Law in the United States, 1867–1973* (1997).

Roe v. Wade (1973), 410 U.S. 113.

Saxon, Wolfgang. 'Henry Wade, Prosecutor in National Spotlight, Dies at 86', *New York Times* (March 2, 2001).

Thornborough v. American College of Obstetricians (1986), 476 US 747.

Webster v. Reproductive Health Services (1989), 492 US 490.

Chapter 9

Billig, Michael. *Rock 'N' Roll Jews* (2000).

Clifford Davis Management v. WEA Records, [1975] 1 WLR 61.

Lloyds Bank v. Bundy, [1975] QB 326.

Macauley v. Schroeder, [1974] 1 WLR 1308.

National Westminster Bank v. Morgan, [1985] AC 686.

'Obituary: Aaron Schroeder', *New York Times*, www.nytimes.com/ 2009/12/06/arts/music/06schroeder.html.

Pao On v. Lau Yiu Long, [1979] 3 All ER 65.

Stratton, John. *Jews, Race, and Popular Music* (2009).

Thal, Spencer N. 'The Inequality of Bargaining Power Doctrine: The Problem of Defining Contractual Unfairness' (1988) 8 *Oxford J. Leg. Stud.*, 17–19.

Trebilcock, M. J. 'The Doctrine of Inequality of Bargaining Power: Post-Benthamite Economics in the House of Lords' (1976) 26 *Univ. Toronto L. J.*, 359.

Chapter 10

Hutchinson, Allan C. *Laughing At The Gods: Great Judges and How They Made the Common Law* (2012).

Lord Sankey in *Edwards*, [1930] AC 124.

Re Same Sex Marriage, [2004] 3 SCR 698.

Warshaw, Matt. *The Encyclopedia Of Surfing* (2005).

INDEX